Benjamin Hall Kennedy

The Revised Version of the New Testament

With an Appendix Containing the Chief Textual Changed

Benjamin Hall Kennedy

The Revised Version of the New Testament
With an Appendix Containing the Chief Textual Changed

ISBN/EAN: 9783337117740

Printed in Europe, USA, Canada, Australia, Japan

Cover: Foto ©Lupo / pixelio.de

More available books at **www.hansebooks.com**

LECTURES
ON THE
REVISED VERSION

ELY LECTURES

ON THE

REVISED VERSION OF THE NEW TESTAMENT

WITH AN APPENDIX

CONTAINING THE CHIEF TEXTUAL CHANGES

BY

B. H. KENNEDY, D.D.

CANON OF ELY AND HON. FELLOW OF ST JOHN'S COLLEGE, CAMBRIDGE

LONDON

RICHARD BENTLEY & SON, NEW BURLINGTON STREET

Publishers in Ordinary to Her Majesty the Queen

1882

All rights reserved

TO THE

REV. F. H. SCRIVENER, LL.D.

&c., &c., &c.

MY DEAR DR. SCRIVENER,

I obtained your kind permission to inscribe to you the three Sermons printed in this volume. They were preached in Ely Cathedral last July; the first of them having been also preached before the University of Cambridge in January 1861.

I wished to express my high esteem for one who has devoted his life to the holy task of purifying the text of the Greek Testament. Others have worked with honour in the same field at the same time, two of whom are gone to their rest, Tregelles and Alford: three survive, Tischendorf, Westcott, Hort. All these, except perhaps Tregelles, were placed in conditions of life more prosperous than yours seemed to be for many years. Happily, your merits have now found a fair recompense of reward, by the act of two truly noble persons; and I cordially wish you long life and health to occupy and enjoy your present sphere of duty.

These sermons I preached during my Ely residence, because I felt that British congregations ought to hear as much as can be told them concerning the need, the conditions, and the execution of the important work which has engaged our revising company more than eleven years.

So far as I have observed, Americans seem to have understood and acknowledged the need of that work more justly than our own countrymen. In America only a few scattered voices, in Great Britain more than a few, have been found to say in print that no work of revision was required, seeing that the Authorised Version is all that can reasonably be desired.

If any sincere Christian holds this opinion, I would say to him, with all respect, 'Study the question well, and you must yield to the force of facts ; or else surrender your prejudice (for judgment it is not) to the verdict of those who have studied that question.' My conviction was gained by Biblical studies in early life, and avowed in my sermon at Cambridge twenty years ago ; but it is not to my verdict, though faithful, that I ask the assent of anti-revising Christians. That verdict has been confirmed by many consentient voices ; by the five clergymen (eminent scholars and divines) who published a revision of several books of the New Testament, by the Southern Convocation of the Anglican Church, when it named a committee to shape this work in

1870; by the Scotch Kirk and the dissenting communities of Great Britain, when they gave representatives to sit in the two revising companies; by Christians in the United States of America, when they established a committee of divines to co-operate with the British revisers. Thus it appears that all English-speaking Christian bodies, except the Roman Catholic, have with united voice acknowledged the necessity and the duty of revision.

If these things do not assure anti-revisers that the work was wanted, let them read and weigh the paper of Dr. Ezra Abbot, the learned American divine, which I reprint in my second Appendix. In this able summary they will find proof, ample and irresistible, that revision was indeed sorely needed; that the means were provided, and the time was ripe; the hour had struck, and the men were ready.

I. From your Cambridge Text of 1881 (supposed to be that followed in 1611), and from Archdeacon Palmer's Text of 1881 (that corrected by the revisers), I derive the following facts—roughly stated, I admit, but with exactness enough for my purpose. The Authorised Text contains about 5,200 readings which the revisers, guided by the comparison of available authorities (manuscripts, versions, and various documentary evidence), have deemed to be erroneous, and have therefore altered. Three-fourths of these alterations do not in any notable respect modify the subject-matter of the sacred writers; but while we rejoice in the general agreement of texts as to fact and doctrine, we ought all to concur in wishing to read as nearly as possible the precise words of the several writers. In the exercise of my fallible judgment, wishing to err on the inclusive side, I have printed in my second Appendix nearly 1,300 varieties of reading which seemed to be in some degree notable. But even of this list it is only a fraction that can be said to have signal importance. I do not presume to settle that fraction; for in doing this the best scholars and divines would assuredly differ among themselves. To their collective deliberation I leave any such judgment.

It may, then, be laid down as an undeniable truth, that the Revised Version represents a Greek text incomparably more pure and nearer to the original than that on which the Authorised Version is founded.

II. The conditions and the execution of our work are correlative topics, and as such must be treated under one head. I am now assisted by the tract of my dear friend Mr. Humphry, which has come into my hands since I preached at Ely, entitled 'One Word on the Revised Version of the New Testament.' I agree with most of what he has written, though, as will later appear, not with every word. He justly says that the governing principle of our work required us 'to make as few changes as possible consistently with faithfulness: changes in the nature of paraphrases or embellishment of style were thus discouraged.' He entirely confirms my language in the third sermon by saying (p. 21), 'Neither I, nor any of my colleagues, is able to stand up for the revision as the product of absolute wisdom. Each of us, times out of number, has been outvoted by a "tyrant majority." There is no sentence in our Preface which had our more hearty approval than that which confesses the existence of blemishes, imperfections, failures; though, if each of us had made out a list of such blots, no two of the lists, probably, would have been found to agree. It cannot be otherwise where many minds are discussing the multifarious details of a long and difficult work, though the advantages arising from their joint counsel greatly outweigh the drawbacks.'

Referring to the passages which he cites (pp. 12, &c.), I agree with him as to Luke xiv. 10; xvi. 9; John i. 25; x. 16; Acts viii. 9, 11, 13; 2 Cor. v. 14; Phil. iii. 21; 1 Tim. vi. 5. I agree also as to Luke xxiii. 15, compared with Matt. v. 21; but he might have strengthened his case by observing that the participle πεπραγμένος favours the instrumental dative, while the aorist ἐρρέθη is more favourable to the objective dative. I agree with him as to the adoption of the name Hades; but I heartily wish Gehenna also had been placed in the text, and for Γέεννα τοῦ πυρός, 'the fiery Gehenna.' It is noticeable that hell (*hölle*, the hidden or dark place) corresponds rather to Hades; but, on account of our existing associations, was properly refused to it. I should feel no regret if the word *hell* were withdrawn from our Testament. The parable in St. Luke xvi. 19, &c., may suffice for those who wish to describe 'the abode of sin' as a place of fire; and the metaphorical use of Gehenna would soon become familiar. Again, I agree very much with Mr. Humphry as to the retention of archaisms generally, and the removal of some. About 'which' or 'who,' when personal, I had my doubts; but I acquiesce in the decision of the majority. I agree, too, in the retention of those Hebraisms which Mr. Humphry cites; but there are some which I should like to have altered, as the 'Gehenna of fire,' and 'the spirit of holiness' (Rom. i. 4), by which rendering of the A. V. the antithesis κατὰ σάρκα—κατὰ πνεῦμα ἁγιωσύνης is made too obscure. Our views of the revised Lord's Prayer in Matt. vi. are nearly similar. But I do not feel the force of his remarks on the petition, 'Thy will,' &c. I always gave to 'as' the simple meaning 'even as,' and was rather disposed to keep the Authorised rendering. About ἀπὸ τοῦ πονηροῦ I have been 'in a strait betwixt two.' Once I voted for placing 'evil one' in the margin; later on, feeling the strength of the argument for the masculine, I did not vote: and I am afraid I still doubt on which side the scale of obligation preponderates. The argument for 'robbers,' as against 'thieves,' in Matt. xxvii. 38, cannot, I think, be resisted. In Matt. xxvi. 22 I decidedly prefer 'is it I, Lord?' to the other order, but from no 'servile adherence to the Greek.' In Mark xv. 37, and Luke xxiii. 46, ἐξέπνευσε, it is, perhaps, vain to plead for the literal 'expired' against the 'solemn old English phrase, gave up the ghost.' Luther renders it in all four Gospels by one word, 'verschied.' In John i. 15 could not γέγονεν have been rendered 'is come to be'? In translating the Theætetus of Plato I have often used this English for γενέσθαι. Τοὺς σωζομένους in Acts ii. is a very trying phrase. What has been chosen in the revision meets the sense, though not all one could wish: I forget whether 'those seeking salvation' was considered or not. We seem to concur as to Acts xxvi. 28, which I do not regard as 'difficult.' But my friend will see that in 29 I agree with Webster and Wilkinson in taking ἐν ὀλίγῳ καὶ ἐν μεγάλῳ with εὐξαίμην ἂν τῷ Θεῷ, which (as ἐν ὀλίγῳ before modifies the act of persuasion, not the quality of χριστιανόν) is manifestly more proper than to carry them on, out of the natural order, to γενέσθαι. The correct rendering of nautical terms in Acts xxvii. is noticed by Mr. Humphry, and generally acknowledged even by adverse critics. The adoption of 'love' for ἀγάπη everywhere, to the exclusion of the word 'charity,' I have defended as certainly right and absolutely necessary; and I suppose that all the revisers, like Mr. Humphry, are of this opinion.

The most important merits of translation are accuracy, neatness, and elegance of style and rhythm.

In accuracy of translation, which, for a book such

as the New Testament, is by far the most valuable quality, no scholar can doubt that the Revised Version is incomparably superior to the Authorised. A few passages there are, upon the interpretation of which the revisers differed among themselves, as Rom. ix. 5 ; 1 Cor. ii. 13 ; Phil. iii. 16 : a few also on which divines outside their body differ from them, as Matt. vi. 13 ; Heb. i. 1 : but these are but slight departures from the general voice of approbation. A few specimens of the two versions, A. and R., compared with each other, must suffice to illustrate this part of my letter.

Matt. i. 18. A., *was espoused*; R., was betrothed. 19. A., *a just man*; R., a righteous man. 22. A., *now all this was done*; R., now all this is come to pass. 25. A., *a virgin*; R., the virgin. ii. 1. A., *there came wise men from the east to Jerusalem*; R., wise men from the east came to Jerusalem. 2. A., *we have seen*; R., we saw. 6. A., *shall rule*; R., shall be shepherd of. 8. A., *that I may come and worship him also*; R., that I also may come and worship him. 16. A., *children*; R., male children. A. *coasts*; R., borders. A., *diligently inquired*; R., carefully learnt. 22. A., *did reign*; R., was reigning. iii. 1. A., *came*; R., cometh. 4. A., *the same John*; R., John himself. 7. A., *came*; R., coming. A., *who hath warned*; R., who warned. 8. A., *meet for repentance*; R., worthy of repentance. 12. A., *purge his floor*; R., cleanse his threshing-floor. 14. A., *John forbade him*; R., John would have hindered him. 16. A., *descending like a dove, and lighting upon him* ; R., descending as a dove, and coming upon him.

As to neatness, I must again be content to quote two or three instances out of the crowd which might easily be gathered from the books at large. Matt. ii. 4. A., *And when he had gathered all the chief priests and scribes of the people together, he demanded of them where Christ should be born* ; R., And gathering together all the chief priests and scribes of the people, he inquired of them where the Christ should be born. (Compare also v. 7, 9, 11.) iv. 3. A., *And when the tempter came to him, he said, If thou be the Son of God, command that these stones be made bread*; R., And the tempter came and said unto him, If thou art the Son of God, command that these stones become bread. 24. A., *And his fame went throughout all Syria: and they brought unto him all sick people that were taken with divers diseases and torments, and those which were possessed with devils, and those which were lunatic, and those that had the palsy; and he healed them* ; R., And the report of him went forth into all Syria ; and they brought unto him all that were sick, holden with divers diseases and torments, possessed with devils, and epileptic, and palsied ; and he healed them. [As larger specimens, Rom. v., or Phil. ii., may be compared in the two versions.]

Style and rhythm are in some degree matters of opinion, and different minds must often agree to differ respecting them. In Matt. v. 26 we have been much censured for writing 'the last farthing' for 'the uttermost farthing' of Auth. V. But without raising the disputable question whether uttermost is, without limitation, a synonym of 'last,' I think it in better taste here to use 'last.' If I had no silver in my purse, I might say, I have used it to the last sixpence; I would not say, 'to the uttermost sixpence.' A severe critic of our grammar and style, writing in 'Public Opinion,' calls us to account for employing an ellipse common to Greek, Latin, and German, as well as to our own tongue—the use of one singular verb with several subjects. Therefore, as to I Cor. xiii. 13, '*νυνὶ δὲ μένει πίστις, ἐλπίς, ἀγάπη, τὰ τρία ταῦτα*—nunc autem manet spes, fides, caritas, tria hæc—nun aber bleibt Glaube, Hoffnung, Liebe, diese drei—but now abideth faith, hope, love, these three'—each version is alike erroneous, alike condemnable, in his judgment. But perhaps the idiom of four concurring languages, represented severally by Paul, Jerome, Luther, and the Revisers of 1611 and 1881, may be a quadrilateral strong enough to sustain, without succumbing, the assault of one modern English grammarian. In Matt. xxii. 40, our defence would have been more complete if, after taking *κρέμαται* for the old reading *κρέμανται*, we had translated in the order of our Greek, 'the whole law hangeth,' instead of 'hangeth the whole law.' The same critic contrasts, to our apparent disadvantage, the two translations, Authorised and Revised, of Matt. xiii. 37–39. Let me set them side by side, as he has done.

Auth.	*Rev.*
He answered and said unto them, He that soweth the good seed is the Son of man; the field is the world; the good seed are the children of the kingdom; but the tares are the children of the wicked one; the enemy that sowed them is the devil; the harvest is the end of the world; and the reapers are the angels.	And he answered and said, He that soweth the good seed is the Son of man; and the field is the world; and the good seed, these are the sons of the kingdom; and the tares are the sons of the evil one; and the enemy that sowed them is the devil; and the harvest is the end of the world; and the reapers are angels.

Here it cannot be denied that the Authorised, by neglecting the particles, has gained a buoyancy and comeliness of form which the Revisers have sacrificed by retaining seven 'ands' instead of one. But what the critic does not notice or suggest is this, that their choice was made with full deliberation, and clear consciousness of its rhetorical disadvantage. The older translators had, in this somewhat exceptional case, thought proper to exhibit a piece of English well pared and neatly trimmed. The Revisers thought it better to retain the peculiar character of St. Matthew's style. A characteristic habit of St. Mark is the frequent 'straightway;' of St. Luke the oft-recurring phrase 'and it came to pass;' in St.

Matthew the superabundant number of connective particles, δέ and καί. The Revisers, as faithful portrait-painters, were minded to retain all these peculiar features. Pedantry there was none in this decision; nor ought such a word ever to have been applied to a body of men so variously trained in different schools and colleges, all of mature age, and most of them long employed in the highest work of English culture. I cannot, however, deny that in the passage last cited there is something to be said in favour of the Authorised Version. It is this:—In the Revised English 'and' is a heavier particle than δέ which it represents; and, as it begins each clause, while δέ is always post-positive, the heaviness of the Revised Version is further increased by this circumstance. For these reasons it is very possible that, if a larger company of Revisers were, as a court of appeal, to review our work on a definite number of disputed points (this being one), a majority might reverse our decision, and vote in this particular case to omit the particles. I have spoken of their omission here by the older translators as an exceptional instance. Comparison of ch. viii. in A. V. will confirm this opinion. Out of thirty-four of its verses, twenty-three begin with 'and,' which occurs forty-three times besides; R. V., maintaining its own principle, begins twenty-nine of the verses with 'and,' and has 'and' forty times additionally.

Having been thus led to speak of a review of our work as an imaginary circumstance, and being so far advanced in years that I cannot expect to see the issue of this momentous enterprise, I venture to ask those who are the proper persons to consider and decide, whether, after the interval of a year, within which time criticism at home and abroad may have said its last word, the Revising Company might not usefully be invited to meet again, and, while they review their reviewers, to review themselves by such light as would have been gained. To what steps such a review might lead, I do not presume, as a single member, to suggest. 'Viderint alii.' Surely a heavy responsibility would rest somewhere, I cannot say where, if the present great opportunity should be frittered away, instead of being improved to the utmost; if Bibles and liturgies containing proved corruptions and errors in important passages were long left to circulate among Christian people, as representing the pure Word of God. To many minds this would seem to be a shame and a scandal.

III. You and I, dear Dr. Scrivener, have sat together eleven years, often voting, like other Revisers, on opposite sides, but without impairing, as I hope and believe, our mutual regard and esteem. My view of Rom. ix. 5 (to which I must now add Tit. ii. 13) has not, as I know, your approval and support. My reasons for it are set forth in Appendix I. to these sermons, and need not be recited here. But, as my friend Mr. Humphry speaks with avowed pleasure of the new rendering adopted in Titus, I am compelled unwillingly to say that I do not share his satisfaction; for I feel morally certain that St. Paul's mind would have been expressed had 'our Saviour' been written (as in A. V.) instead of Saviour alone, or if, to avoid all doubt, it had been placed at the close of the sentence, 'the great God and Jesus Christ our Saviour.' In another place (p. 15) Mr. Humphry justly deprecates 'a servile adherence to the order of the Greek;' I do the same here. I would give to Σωτῆρος a capital Σ: and as to the absence of the article τοῦ, after having rendered Ἁγίου Πνεύματος in Matt. i. 20, and Ἅγιον Πνεῦμα in Luke ii., '*the* Holy Ghost,' besides other places in which we have supplied a definite article, there was no occasion to avoid a like freedom here. Therefore, if on doctrinal grounds I thought it important to argue that St. Paul does not give to our Saviour the predicate Θεός, I should refuse to acknowledge either passage, Rom. or Tit., as valid proof against me. But I have no such interest. I accept with reverent assent the decrees of Nicæa and Constantinople, and the definitions of the later creed, 'Quicunque vult,' as logically just deductions from the teaching of Holy Scripture, thus adhering to the sixth Article of my Church as well as to the first and eighth. Therefore my orthodoxy cannot be impugned by authority. It may be impugned unauthoritatively by those who have persuaded themselves that the writers of Holy Scripture were not only guarded by the Holy Spirit from all noxious error, but also guided into all truth in heaven and earth. I do not share this opinion. St. Paul calls θεότης a mystery (1 Tim. iii. 16); he calls Christ Himself the mystery of God (Col. i. 27; ii. 2); he speaks of Christ Jesus (Phil. ii) as ἐν μορφῇ Θεοῦ ὑπάρχων, and (equivalently) as ὢν ἴσα Θεῷ: he says (Col. ii. 9) that in Christ dwells all the fulness of θεότης in bodily form: but when to the Christian Jews of Rome (Rom. i. 3, 4) he describes Him solemnly as the subject of his gospel, how does he speak of Him? As Son, 'born of the seed of David according to the flesh, but according to His divine spirit (κατὰ πνεῦμα ἁγιωσύνης) defined to be the Son of God.' As Paul in these great places, and in so many others, has refrained from predicating Christ as θεός, I do not think he did so in two dubious places, confessedly capable of being otherwise explained. Even St. John, who has in his opening chapter θεὸς ἦν ὁ Λόγος, and perhaps even μονογενὴς θεός, in allusion to Christ, does not repeat the same elsewhere. Hence I do not think that any apostle, John, or Peter, or Paul, was so taught the full μυστήριον θεότητος as that they were prepared to formulate the decrees of Nicæa and Constantinople, which appeared after 300 years and more, or the Trinitarian exegesis, which was completed after 600 years and more. But they, with the other evangelists, guided by the Holy Spirit, furnished the materials from which those doctrines were developed. What then? Are we better off than they by virtue of our Trinitarian logic? In point of *practice*, not a whit. They knew all that was needed to make them love Christ as human and *divine*, to worship him as *divine*. Can we *practically* do more? They knew that they had received the Divine Spirit, and they could pray for the continuance of His gifts, individually and in communion. Can we *practically* do more? Happy we if we *practically* do as much. And, after all, what are our dogmas περὶ θεότητος, concerning the divine 'modus existendi'? If we examine them with care, we shall find them, mainly, logical negations, however important and valuable for repelling error. We see God δι' ἐσόπτρου ἐν αἰνίγματι. If we believe in Him, hope in Him, love Him, as shown to us in Christ Jesus σωματικῶς, the τότε will come in His good time, when we shall see Him πρόσωπον πρὸς πρόσωπον. Meanwhile the Nicene Creed, the creed 'Quicunque vult,' the Anglican and other Articles, are, on this subject, ἐκ μέρους. Till *then* 'we know in part, and we prophesy in part: but when that which is perfect is come, that which is in part shall be done away.' 'Although' (says Hooker) ' to know God be life, and joy to make mention of His name, yet our soundest knowledge is to know that we know Him not as indeed He is, neither can know Him: and our safest eloquence concerning Him is our silence, when we confess, without confession, that His glory is inexplicable, His greatness above our capacity and reach. He is above, and we upon earth; therefore it behoveth our words to be wary and few.'

If you find my letter too discursive, ascribe this fault to my loyal zeal for the success of a great work in which I have had but a small share, while your part in it has been large and important.

I am, my dear Dr. Scrivener,

Yours most sincerely,

B. H. KENNEDY.

CONTENTS.

SERMON I.
The Interpretation of the Bible . . . 1

SERMON II.
The Revised Text . . . 30

SERMON III.
The Revised Version . . . 52

APPENDICES.

Appendix I. 75
Appendix II. 91
Appendix III.: Select Textual Correction . 101

Postscript . . . 155
Note . . . 161

SERMON I.

THE INTERPRETATION OF THE BIBLE.[1]

1 CORINTHIANS II. 15.

The spiritual man judgeth all things.

I. IF we regard man as a free moral agent, and religion as the method ordained by God to restore him to his Maker's image, lost by sin, it is evident that in every religious transaction there are two factors operating, the divine and the human. The mutual and the joint operation of these factors we cannot measure, because the divine nature and its workings lie beyond the reach of human definition. We know only what is revealed to us of them in the Word of God, and what we are allowed to see of their results in the lives and characters of men. The highest phase of this truth—the sun, as it were,

[1] Parts I. and II. of this Sermon were preached before the University of Cambridge in January 1862. Parts I. and III. were preached in Ely Cathedral in July 1881.

B

from which all its exhibitions radiate—is the great doctrine of the Incarnation, very God and very man united in one Christ. The man Christ Jesus was thereby constituted the one Mediator between God and man. The possibility of man's reunion with God was objectively declared, and the means of realising it subjectively were brought within man's reach. In all these means the concurrence of the divine and human factors is again supposed. If we are saved by grace on the part of God, it is through faith on our own part. If the Spirit beareth witness, it is with our spirits. If we work out our own salvation, it is while God worketh in us both to will and to do. If we pray, it is because prayer is the voice of faith, appointed to receive the answering grace of God. And the Sacraments were ordained by Christ, partly indeed to knit His servants together by common pledges of Christian brotherhood, but partly, too, as solemn acts, wherein divine grace and human faith should meet and co-operate with mysterious power and effect.

When we review the various heresies[1] which from time to time have divided the Christian

---

[1] The term 'heresy' is used in its ancient Scriptural sense as a sect or form of doctrine.

Church, and those which yet divide it, we perceive that most of them arise from the exaggeration of one of these elements of religious truth and action, to the consequent depreciation of the other element.

Thus, in regard to the first and cardinal doctrine—the nature of our blessed Saviour—the Ebionite heresy, since called Socinian, utterly denied His divine nature; while the Arian and semi-Arian heresies disparaged it in various degrees. On the other hand, the Doketic heresy annihilated our Lord's human nature; and the Apollinarian, Monophysite, and Monotheletic heresies, severally, mutilated that human nature in some function. It stands to reason, that all erroneous teaching in regard to the nature of our Lord and Saviour Jesus Christ becomes, in its place and proportion, erroneous teaching in regard to that work of human redemption which was wrought indeed, objectively as to each of us, by Him alone, but wrought by Him as very God and very man, united in one Christ.

If we next look to the work of individual salvation, in which the divine and the human concur and co-operate, it will again appear, on the face of history, that error has arisen, generally, from the exaggeration of the one element to the disparagement of the other. Thus Pelagius overrated man's natural powers as a moral agent, and so detracted from the converting and regenerating grace of the Holy Spirit. On the other side the element of human freedom has been ignored by Calvinistic excess; and though it were improper to say that divine prescience and power have been overrated, we may say it has been forgotten that the finite mind has no measure for qualities infinitely residing in God, and no faculty of comprehending, what nevertheless it should believe, their harmonious coexistence and perfect reconciliation in Him.

The same kind of error meets us again in the opinions which have been held concerning the Sacraments. The Romanist, on the one hand, infers grace from the outward work alone, to the neglect of human faith: the Zwinglian, on the other, treats them as mere acts of human obedience, having no promise of special grace.

What then, it will naturally be asked, is our test of truth in these questions, and what our rule of duty? Surely it is our wisdom to believe that each of these doctrines is a great and holy mystery, which we can see only in part, and concerning which we can prophesy only in part, while we are yet clothed with this body of decay and death. Surely it is our duty to accept fully, and fully, as far as we are enabled, to act upon, both those elements which Holy Scripture shows to us as coexisting and co-operating; and not to beat our wings against the cage, wasting our moral and intellectual strength in controversies, of which we 'find no end, in wandering mazes lost.' Such controversies, alas! are often worse than unpractical; they have proved, and in some cases still prove, to be 'logomachies, of which cometh envy, strife, railings, evil surmisings.' Let us escape from them by use of the clue which our Church has wisely and kindly given in her 17th Article, ' receiving God's promises in such wise as they be generally set forth to us in Holy Scripture, and, in our doings, following that will of God which we have expressly declared unto us in the Word of God.'

There are two other important and mutually related questions of religion, in which again we have to recognise the presence of the divine and human factors, without venturing to determine the precise mode and degree in which they severally operate. These questions are the inspiration and the interpretation of the Holy Scriptures.

Divine inspiration is a property, expressly ascribed by St. Paul to the writings of the Old Testament, and justly inferred of those of the New, from our Saviour's promises, and from the character of the writers. Attempt has often been made, and still is made, to define the manner and extent of this inspiration. No such attempt has been established as a norm in the Church, and we verily believe that, as elsewhere, so here, the nature of the case precludes accurate definition. The nearest approach to a rule will probably be that which shall most distinctly recognise the constant presence of the Holy Spirit with the sacred writers, without denying the free development of their human faculties in the work of authorship. 'It seemed good to the Holy Ghost and to us,' said the apostles in their first council; thus claiming the sanction of the Holy Ghost for the collective decision of their inspired minds, and yet expressing their individual judgment as persons who had exercised free thought and discussion.[1]

[1] The notion of '*verbal*' inspiration, not yet abandoned universally, is too palpably absurd to require serious refutation. If the authors were thus prompted, what of the countless transcribers and translators, whose varying copies are received as

The broad principles of Biblical interpretation are analogous to those of inspiration. The Bible is to be interpreted by the employment of the human faculties under divine assistance and direction. We place no limit to the use of man's learning, acuteness, and industry, as means to an end, in determining the text of the Bible, and in ascertaining its sense, grammatically, logically, historically; but after all—confronting the charge of mysticism, which we expect from the worshippers of human reason—we say that spiritual things can be fully explained by the Spirit alone; and that, consequently, none but spiritual men are qualified to form an accurate judgment of the great truths of salvation.

Let us turn our attention now to the very important passage in which my text occurs.

In his First Epistle to the Corinthians, St. Paul, after reproving the Christians of Corinth for their sectarian divisions, reminds them that he himself had preached to them the plain vital doctrine of Christ and Him crucified, a stumblingblock to the Jews, who desired a sign—that

Holy Writ? Of every Bible it may be said, 'Herein is divine truth, but alloyed with human error, which we must strive to clear away by all the means given to us for the welfare of our souls.'

is, a striking manifestation of power; and foolishness to the Greeks, who loved philosophic speculation. At Corinth St. Paul had chiefly to dread the Greek error. He therefore goes on to say that, in setting forth the doctrine of Christ and Him crucified, he had purposely abstained from the rhetorical display of mere human learning, that he might more distinctly exhibit the power of the Holy Spirit. Yet (he says) I preach a true wisdom, hidden from the great ones of this world, but revealed to Christians by the Spirit of God; for 'the Spirit searcheth all things, yea, the deep things of God.'

The passage, which all but follows, extending from the 12th verse of the second to the 4th verse of the third chapter, I will now venture to read, with that amount of paraphrase, and those variations from the Authorised Version, which are required to exhibit the view I have been led to take of its meaning.

'Now we apostles of Christ received not that inspiration which men of the world receive, making them subtle disputants, eloquent speakers, and fine writers, but the inspiration which is from God; that we may know the blessings bestowed upon us by the grace of

God. And these things we speak in words not taught of human wisdom, but taught of divine inspiration, explaining spiritual things to spiritual men. For the natural (that is, the merely intellectual) man receiveth not the things of the Spirit of God, for they are foolishness unto him: neither can he know them, because they are to be judged in a spiritual manner. But the spiritual man is able to form a judgment on all these points, while the natural man has no power to judge him. For who, as Isaiah says, knoweth the mind or spirit of the Lord, so that he shall instruct Him? And we who are true Christians have that mind or spirit of the Lord Christ. So that no natural man can correct us. And yet, brethren, I could not speak to you as to spiritual men, but I had to speak to you as carnal men, as infant Christians. I fed you with milk, not with meat, for hitherto ye could not bear it. Nor can ye now: for ye are yet carnal. For whereas there is among you jealousy and strife, are ye not carnal, and walking in the steps of unrenewed man?'

St. Paul, in short, says that the power which the Spirit gives to a Christian is something different from mere human power: that it makes him able to understand, and, if a preacher, to explain spiritual things: but that his hearers cannot understand him unless they too are spiritual: and, in so far as they are still carnal, they must be reared and trained in elementary doctrines like infants, till the mind of Christ be developed within them.

By the psychic or natural man St. Paul means the unconverted possessor of mere human learning and science, having specially in view the Greek philosopher. He does not intend to say that the Christian can acquire no useful knowledge from an infidel (for indeed we may learn Hebrew from the Jew or Arabic from the Mahometan); but he implies that the infidel, to whom the faith and hope and love of the Christian are known only by name, can form no just notion of the Christian character, and contribute nothing to its instruction, edification, and completion. In respect to Biblical interpretation, the infidel may, perchance, assist us to explain the letter, but he can throw no light on the spirit, of the Bible.

Again, we find Christians themselves cited by the apostle in this place under three several heads or classes. First, we have spiritual men who, like St. Paul and his fellow-labourers, speak and explain spiritual things: next, we have spiritual men to whom such things are explained, and who are competent to form a right judgment thereof: and lastly, we have infant Christians, babes in Christ, whom the apostle could not address as spiritual, but as carnal; yet Christians still, and included among those whom, in his preface, St. Paul had termed 'the Church of God, called to be saints.'

Now (to speak of the last class in the first place) does not the language of St. Paul in dealing with such men teach the same doctrine which we learn from our Lord's parables of the tares, the net, and the vine: the same which we deduce also from the presence of a traitor among His disciples: namely, that those who have been received into the Church, though they be carnal, are not on that account to be dealt with as heathens, but to be corrected, strengthened, and restored, if so it may be, by wise and kind discipline? We should further observe, that all professing Christians are in charity to be considered and dealt with as spiritual men, except so far as they give by their walk and conduct unquestionable evidence of being carnal. St. Paul does not speak to these Corinthians as being carnal and not spiritual, without stating his grounds for so speaking : 'There is jealousy and strife among you.' Never, never let us lay a snare for the conscience of a Christian brother by requiring of him any other test of spirituality than that of Christian conduct, which our Saviour has sanctioned : 'By their fruits ye shall know them.' When plain proof of carnality is absent, let us hope all things of their spiritual state, judging not, that we be not judged.

For let us not extend too widely the meaning and application of our text. A Roman Pope, Boniface VIII., had the hardihood to claim for the Roman See supreme jurisdiction in all causes, civil as well as ecclesiastical, by virtue of the maxim that 'the spiritual man judgeth all things.' His successor in our days may perhaps have founded upon the same maxim the right of promulgating a new dogma of Christian faith without the sanction of a General Council.[1] We mention such extravagances only to show to what extent the Bible has been, and may be, misinterpreted by erring

---

[1] The allusion here is to the dogma of the ' Immaculate Conception of the Virgin,' sanctioned by Pope Pius IX. This claim he subsequently carried to its fatal extreme, by obtaining, in 1869, the sanction of what he was pleased to call a General Council, to the doctrine (till then repudiated by all but the Jesuits) of Papal Infallibility.

men. Here the term 'all things,' whether it have the Greek article or not, evidently implies all those things, mentioned above, which God has freely given to them that love Him. These are the things explained by the spiritual preacher; these are the things of which the spiritual hearer can form a judgment; not the mind and the heart of a Christian brother: for God alone knoweth the hearts of men. With respect to those spiritual men, whose office it is in these times to follow St. Paul and the other apostles in explaining spiritual things to the spiritual, earnestly must we desire, earnestly should we pray, that they may be spiritual indeed, preserved by the Holy Spirit from all error and evil, guided into all truth, and enabled to preach the word with power. Yet we are not entitled to rank the very best among them —they certainly would not rank themselves— with a Paul, an Apollos, and a Cephas; even as a Paul, an Apollos, and a Cephas would not rank themselves with Christ. We dare not class the words of any fallible men at any time since the apostolic age—be the speakers ever so good and wise and learned and weighty— with the inspired oracles of God. When such men speak, let us hear with reverent attention, but, if doubt arise, we must search the Scriptures, as did the Beræans, to see whether these things be so. We must search the Scriptures with diligent and thoughtful study, yet with deep humility and with constant prayer. For in this work the divine and human must go together. The spiritual man alone is competent to form a correct judgment of spiritual things. By the sanctified soul the saving truths of the Gospel will be more distinctly and fully seen than by the larger learning of the merely intellectual student. Yet the admission of this principle, rightly viewed, has no tendency to discourage or disparage the value of human learning and talent and industry in the study of the Bible. For the truly spiritual man is an humble, a zealous, a conscientious man; and in each character he will neglect no means which God has placed within his reach of acquainting both himself and others with the truth as it is in Jesus.

As regards the textual constitution, the grammatical and logical explanation, of the New Testament, we must admit that new results are from time to time achieved by improved learning and enlarged research. And, as lovers of truth (for, if not such, we are very unworthy servants of Him who is the truth as well as the life), we ought to lament that these results were so long restricted to the use of the professed divine, instead of being made, as soon as possible, the common property of Christians. Do we not still see the spurious verse of St. John's first epistle (1 John v. 7) cited as genuine, by writers of slender learning, it is true, but for that very reason, perhaps, the more popular in an age of shallow reading? Is not St. Paul's evidence still quoted in terms which he did not use: '*God* was manifest in the flesh'? And are not the great divine truths themselves liable to be injured by this abuse, when the student discovers that texts which he has been wont to hear cited as normal are not Biblical texts at all? Yet superficial or bigoted minds may still claim the right of quoting these texts, as long as the Church sets them before her children as genuine portions of the sacred volume.

II. An eminent writer of the day very justly cautions his readers against the idle or fallacious use of Scriptural language. One such instance I have given in the misapplication of the words of my text by Pope Boniface. But indeed of such misapplications the name is legion. What text is oftener cited and preached upon than the words 'Search the Scriptures'? yet the logic of the context requires us to read, 'Ye search the Scriptures:' and we fear the translators were dazzled by the apparent value of the imperative sense as a weapon against Romanism. 'Comparing spiritual things with spiritual' were the words prefixed to the Sermons on Scripture coincidences by one whose memory we all revere and love. My view of the context has obliged me to render the Greek otherwise: 'explaining spiritual things to spiritual men:' as in the 1st verse of the twelfth chapter the context again induces me to read 'spiritual persons' rather than 'spiritual things.' The value of Professor Blunt's sermons was altogether independent of his text: but his high sanction seemed to be given to an erroneous translation. Far more momentous was the error of the great Augustine, when, being ignorant of Greek, and following the Latin Vulgate, he argued the imputation of Adam's sin to his descendants from a mistranslation of the 12th verse of the fifth chapter of Romans; rendering 'in whom all sinned' instead of 'inasmuch as all sinned.'—Take another instance. The very words of St. Paul in this Epistle to the Corinthians,—'we preach Christ crucified,' and again,

'I determined not to know any thing among you, save Jesus Christ, and Him crucified,'—in how many sermons have they been made a groundwork for the doctrine of the Atonement, as the great cardinal work of Christ! Yet these texts afford no basis either for that doctrine itself, or for its claim to supreme importance in Christ's redeeming work. St. Paul means to aver that he has preached the truth as it is in Jesus fully and honestly, not hiding or sophisticating it to flatter human prejudice. Had his gainsayers been Sadducees, he would perhaps have said, 'We preach Christ, and Him risen from the dead.' As they are proud Pharisaic Jews, and proud intellectual Greeks, he says, we preach Christ, and Him crucified, however offensive to some, and foolish to others, this doctrine of a crucified King and Saviour may appear. The great lesson which St. Paul so teaches these proud men is—that of self-humiliation in face of the true power and wisdom of God: even as in his second chapter to the Philippians the lesson he teaches is that of self-sacrifice, in view of the great example of Christ. 'Let this mind, this unselfish sympathetic mind, be in you, which was also in Christ Jesus, who, subsisting in the form of God, deemed not the being like God a miser's treasure, a thing not to be parted with; but put off His dignity by taking a servant's form, being born in human semblance: and when He was so found as a man in outward guise, He humbled Himself yet further, and became submissive even unto death, and that death the shameful and bitter death of the cross.'

If we turn to the Epistle to the Romans, chap. viii. 33, 34, we shall see (I venture to think) that the clauses rendered in our version 'It is God that justifieth,' 'it is Christ that died,' should have the interrogative form, 'Will God that justifieth' (accuse them)? 'will Christ that died' (condemn them)?

Proceeding to Phil. iii. 16, I cannot but believe that this verse ought to be taken as a preamble to the 17th: 'Nevertheless, seeing we have thus far attained (in our lessons of Christian duty)—to walk by the same rule—be ye with one consent imitators of me,' &c.

It must be admitted that some translations in our English Bible have a purely ecclesiastical character; that is, they have been accommodated to some doctrine which hearers and readers in later times would recognise, but which was certainly not recognised by those to whom the words were first spoken. Such are the passages Matt. i. 18, Luke i. 35, where the phrase 'Pneuma hagion' (holy Spirit) is rendered 'the Holy Ghost.' Whether this rendering, in the absence of the article, is ungrammatical or not, I shall not pretend to determine. Middleton condemns it. But we must surely allow it to be unhistorical. The doctrine of the Holy Trinity, and of the Holy Ghost as the Third Person in the Godhead, was not known to Joseph and Mary, who are severally addressed by the angel in these passages. By 'holy Spirit' they would naturally understand 'a divine inspiration or influence,' that 'power of the Highest' by which the angel virtually interprets the phrase in the passage of Luke. 'Holy Spirit of God' might with advantage replace the words 'Holy Ghost.'

In Rom. ix. 3–5 we read in our Bibles the following words: 'For I could wish that myself were accursed from Christ for my brethren, my kinsmen according to the flesh: who are Israelites; to whom pertaineth the adoption, and the glory, and the covenants, and the giving of the law, and the service of God, and the promises; whose are the fathers, and of whom as concerning the flesh Christ came, who is over all, God blessed for ever.' If this version be correct, then we have here the only place in which St. Paul has said of our Lord Jesus Christ, in express predication, that 'He is God,' and with the strong addition and ascription, 'over all, blessed for ever.' It seems quite incredible that the apostle would choose, for such a momentous isolated declaration, a place like this, where he is consoling the Jews by an enumeration of the special privileges which belonged to them as Jews, the last of these being that from among them should arise the Christ, the Messiah. For to suppose that the final words describe this Christ as God would then necessarily imply that the Jews expected their Messiah to be 'God over all, blessed for ever;' an expectation which they certainly did not entertain, for it would seem to them then (as it seems now) at variance with their fundamental doctrine: 'Hear, O Israel; the Lord your God is one God.' And the modification of this doctrine in the Christian Creed Paul would surely not introduce here without some previous preparation, without some fuller explanation. This rendering we must therefore regard as one of an ecclesiastical character, adopted with too much eagerness, in order to obtain for an important doctrine of the Creed another positive sanction. I entertain little doubt that the words 'Christ came' should be followed by a full stop; the next clause, an ascription of glory, being rendered, 'He who is over all is God, blessed for ever. Amen.'

Biblical criticism, my brethren, is among the most sacred duties of the Christian scholar: a duty to be discharged frankly and faithfully, as under the eye of God. Faithless criticism may be learned, may be sagacious, may often be overruled by God to expose falsehood or to suggest and illustrate truth; but as it is without the divine element, it sees and knows nothing of divine things. The blind cannot lead the blind. Faithless criticism is of the earth, earthy: it seems to flourish and flaunt for a while, but its fashion soon passeth away. The cold and perverse rationalism of Semler and his school, the ingenious dreams of Strauss and the Hegelians —where are they now? They are gone like the chaff which the wind scattereth; and the truth as it is in Jesus is a glad sound once more in the fatherland of Luther and Melancthon.

The spiritual man judgeth all things. Brethren of the laity, it is your privilege and your duty to study in the Bible, to hear from the pulpit, the blessings bestowed upon you by the grace of God. Be spiritual men. So shall ye be able to judge spiritually what ye read and hear, taking heed how ye read and how ye hear. Brethren of the clergy, and ye who are looking forward to the sacred office, it is, or it may be, your high privilege and duty to explain spiritual things. Be spiritual men. So alone will ye be able to divide rightly the word of truth, and to minister grace unto your hearers.

Be spiritual men. But how? In part by humbly believing and remembering that the answer to this question is a mystery. 'The wind bloweth where it listeth, and ye hear the sound thereof, but ye cannot tell whence it cometh, or whither it goeth: even so is every man that is born of the Spirit.' In part by neglecting none of the means of grace prepared for Christians in the Church of Christ—prayer, worship, and the communion of the body and blood of Christ. In part by being willing— willing in heart, willing in body, soul, and mind —to do the will of the Father, and to work out your own salvation with fear and trembling, yea, with the deepest humility, because it is God that worketh in you both to will and to do of His good pleasure. In part also by remembering that spiritual grace is not given at once in its full proportion; that, to be maintained, it must be improved; that we must not stand still, if we would not go backward; that the Christian life, as described in the Epistle for this day's service, is a race for the prize of an imperishable crown, and they who run it must be temperate in all things. Most of all must those be temperate whose high and hard and most responsible function it is to explain spiritual things, lest that by any means, when they have preached unto others, they themselves should be cast away.

May the Holy Spirit breathe upon our distracted Church, and create in it spiritual ministers and spiritual congregations, that carnal jealousies and strifes may die away, and all things belonging to the Spirit may live and grow amongst us: that each Christian may be one with Christ, and all Christians one in Christ; and that Christ Himself, our incarnate Mediator, our crucified Redeemer, our risen Head, our glorified and reigning King, may be all in all, to the glory of God the Father! Amen.[1]]

[1] This concludes the sermon as preached before the University of Cambridge in January 1861.

III. My brethren, the words which I have so far addressed to you are my own words, though read from a printed volume. The sermon to which they belong was preached by me in the University pulpit at Cambridge, on January 27, 1861, more than twenty years ago. At that time I little guessed that a revision would be undertaken in my lifetime, and that I myself should be called to take part in the execution of such a work. Yet that work has been undertaken, has been completed in the course of eleven years and a half, and the new version so revised has now for many weeks been before the eyes of the Scripture-reading public of Great Britain and America. It is at this moment, and for a long time yet it may continue to be, subject to a storm of criticism, of which we must wait to see the consistency, the scope, and the reasons, before we can attempt to organise a defence, and to obtain a fair hearing before the tribunals of sound learning, upright intelligence, and enlightened wisdom.

Meanwhile it is well that English congregations should learn as much as can be told them from the pulpit about this important volume: why it was wanted, what it does to meet that want, and in what respects it is adapted to promote true religion; and its faults (for what human work is faultless?) should be noted with a view to correction. As the volume is printed and published in several sizes, and at varied prices, it is fairly within the reach of all readers except the very poorest; and I may venture to hope that most of those who hear me will soon become acquainted with it, and by studying its clear and careful preface will learn all they ought to know respecting its origin, its design, and the general rules by which the revisers have been guided in the performance of their work.

As one of the revisers, I stand in a delicate position when I venture to add anything to what is said by our collective voice in that preface. But our excellent chairman, the Bishop of Gloucester and Bristol, has spoken more fully on the subject from his place in Convocation. I have read what he there said, which of course forms part of the stock of public information. It is well known that our whole company consisted of some twenty-five or twenty-six members, resident in various parts of Great Britain, engaged in various public duties, and not all of them always able to attend the meetings in the Jerusalem Chamber, which were held on forty days of every year. The average attendance might be about seventeen members, but I speak without certain knowledge, and from mere conjecture. The members unable to attend were at liberty to communicate their opinions in writing on any passages which specially interested them, and such communications always received very careful attention. A committee of American divines was in session at New York for the purpose of regular communication with us. Their notes were sent across the Atlantic, printed, circulated, read, and carefully discussed in our meetings. Our whole work was gone over twice with thorough deliberation; all differences of opinion were settled by the votes of the members present, and in the second revision a majority of two-thirds was required to overrule the Authorised Version if any member thought proper to demand that advantage. It is important for you to observe that the marginal renderings introduced by the conjunction *or* always represent the opinion of a minority present, though such a margin was not necessarily granted, and the minority, when very small, rarely asked for it.

Personally speaking (and I am sure every

reviser would say the same thing) I do not feel myself at liberty, as a loyal comrade, to say where I voted with the majority, where with the minority; that is, I cannot loyally call in question the decisions of the company. But I am in a peculiar position on account of this sermon, in the course of which I expressed opinions on a certain number of passages in the Authorised Version. Some of those opinions are recognised as just by the changes made in revision; others appear in the margin; one or two have gained no recognition. But all these opinions, deliberately formed and expressed twenty years ago, I have not changed. I hold them still. A short time before the close of our labours I called the attention of the company to this sermon, desiring to know whether, in publicly maintaining opinions publicly expressed long ago, without any reference to a revised version, I should be in any respect violating my loyal duty as a reviser. No formal answer could be given to this question, but not a voice was raised in contradiction to the language of the chairman, which intimated that no such imputation could attach to me for so acting. It is not my purpose to bring forward any of those passages now, saving only that one which grows out of the text, viz. 1 Cor. i. 13, 'Interpreting or explaining spiritual things to spiritual men.' This rendering stands in our margin. I would have wished it in the text, because I think that the two following verses imperiously call for it—in fact, prove and enforce its truth. This, I say, is the only instance in which I shall express a dissentient private judgment to-day. I do so because it cannot be well helped, because it is in print already, and because I feel myself licensed to express this opinion without infringement of loyal duty.

In my next discourse I hope to bring to your notice the manner in which the revisers have done the work entrusted to them—the reconstitution, that is, of the Authorised Version. This will lead us to consider two points: first, our corrections of that Greek text which the companies of 1611 followed in translating; secondly, our corrections of the Authorised Version itself, adopted as either essential or desirable.

But while I invite you to hear what I have to say upon the right interpretation of those Holy Scriptures which are profitable for instruction in righteousness, and able, if rightly used, to make us wise unto salvation, I must not part from you at this time without recalling our blessed Lord's warning words, 'Take heed how ye hear.' Bear in mind the maxim of St. Paul in my text: 'The spiritual man judgeth all things.' You cannot judge aright without being spiritual men. You cannot be spiritual men without the grace of God's Holy Spirit. That grace you cannot hope to obtain without using the means appointed to that end, among which are the study of God's Word, even of the truth as it is in Jesus, and the practice of private as well as public prayer. Search the Scriptures, then; pray earnestly: pray especially for me, that I may be empowered to speak to you as a spiritual teacher; pray for yourselves, that you may be enabled to judge my words as spiritual hearers.

SERMON II.

THE REVISED TEXT.

St. John's Gospel xix. 22.

Pilate answered, What I have written I have written.

I. You know, my Christian friends, what Pilate had written, and for what purpose he wrote. Most of you can travel back in thought to that 'place of a skull' near the city of Jerusalem, where about eighteen centuries and a half ago there was standing a wooden cross, to which were nailed the hands—upon which was stretched the tortured body—from which drooped the still bleeding brow—of Him whom the Roman centurion on guard pronounced to be surely the Son of God: of Him, in remembrance of whose sacrifice for your sake many of you here present have received in faith with thanksgiving those consecrated elements of bread and wine, which His priests administer with solemn prayer that the body of Jesus Christ given for you, and the blood of Jesus Christ shed for you, may preserve your bodies and souls unto everlasting life.

Pilate had written an inscription to be placed upon that ever-memorable cross, to be seen above the bleeding head of that tortured body.

Varied as are the Gospel narratives of the deed wrought on that great Good Friday (and in this variety we see the proof of their veracity), they are all agreed in commemorating this inscription. One Evangelist indeed commemorates it more fully than the other three: his Gospel was written long after theirs; but he had been an eye-witness of the scene. For he it was who had leaned on his Master's bosom at the Last Supper: he had stood beside the cross of Jesus: he was the disciple whom Jesus loved, to whom Jesus entrusted His mother: he was the apostle of love, the preacher of Ephesus, the aged exile of Patmos, St. John, the son of Zebedee.

St. Matthew writes:
> 'And they set up over His head His accusation written, This is Jesus the King of the Jews.'

St. Mark:
> 'And the superscription of the accusation

was written over, The King of the Jews.'

In St. Luke we read:

'And the soldiers also mocked Him, coming to Him, offering Him vinegar, and saying, If Thou be the King of the Jews, save Thyself. And there was also a superscription over Him: This is the King of the Jews.'

St. John's account is:

'And Pilate wrote a title also, and put it on the cross. And there was written, Jesus of Nazareth the King of the Jews. This title therefore read many of the Jews; for the place where Jesus was crucified was near to the city: and it was written in Hebrew, and in Latin, and in Greek. The chief priests of the Jews therefore said to Pilate, Write not The King of the Jews; but that he said, I am King of the Jews. Pilate answered, What I have written I have written.'

Why have I called to your minds this inscription to-day? Not in order to dwell now on the divine work then finished, with its mighty causes and consequences. Not to draw moral warnings from the sin of the wicked Jews, or from that of Pilate, in whose conduct and words we may surely trace indignation against the men who had forced his hand, indignation against himself for consenting to so heinous a crime as the murder of One in whom he found no fault. Of these things I have treated in other sermons which the volume, now placed on the shelves of yonder library, contains.

I cite this inscription as well suited to introduce the subject on which I pledged myself to preach this morning, if permitted. I mean the text from which our New Testament has been translated into so many languages besides our own.

Pilate's inscription was couched in three languages—Hebrew, Latin, and Greek. Hebrew, I need hardly say, is the language of the Jews, that in which the books of the Old Testament are written. When our Saviour was on earth, the vulgar speech of the Jewish people had fallen off from the old and classical Hebrew to become a corrupt dialect, known as Syro-Chaldaic or Aramaic, which bore to the language of Moses and David the same sort of relation that the modern Hindustani

D

and Bengali bear to the older language of Hindustan, called Sanscrit.

Pilate's inscription was therefore written in Hebrew, that is, in the common dialect of the Jewish populace, that it might be read by them. Probably he knew little of it himself beyond a smattering of the most usual Aramaic words. His conversations with eminent Jews would be held in a language known to both parties—I mean the Greek.

The Latin language, that of Rome, was the language of the governor, of his staff, and many among his soldiers. It was the official language of Roman government, and would not be omitted by Pilate. But the Jews, I fancy, would have none of it, or as little as could be helped.

There remains the third language used in this inscription, the Greek. This, the finest and most flexible speech the world has ever known, was propagated throughout the whole East then known to Europeans, from the Dardanelles to the Persian Gulf, by means of the wonderful conquests of Alexander the Great, 330 years before the Christian era. In the kingdoms of Egypt and Syria, which were founded by the successors of Alexander, and flourished for a few centuries, Greek was the language of the conquerors, and became to a great extent the language of their subjects. This result the eminently literary and commercial spirit of Greek populations contributed powerfully to achieve. The Jews indeed were what the Books of Maccabees show them; what they remained under the Romans; what they remained through the Middle Ages; what they remain to this day—a peculiar people, fond of their own language, their own religion, their own rites and customs. But Greeks, with the Greek tongue, Greek dress, Greek commerce, Greek habits and influences, were around them everywhere, in Alexandria, Antioch, Damascus, Tyre, and Sidon. Greeks were among them in Palestine, especially in Jerusalem itself, and in trading seaports like Joppa and Cæsarea. The Hebrew Scriptures themselves had been translated into Greek by Jews who had migrated to Egypt, and, becoming familiar with the Greek tongue, were employed by Ptolemy Philadelphus to execute this work. A fabulous tale respecting the manner of its execution by seventy-two translators working separately caused this translation to be generally known as the Septuagint Version. Such Jews as returned to Palestine, especially to Jerusalem itself, speaking Greek and living in Greek fashion, were called Hellenists. In the Acts they are called 'they that fear God.' By such Hellenistic Jews were written in Greek those Apocryphal books which our Church, by her 6th Article, allows to be read for example of life and instruction of manners, but does not receive as a rule of faith.

Thus you see that it was quite necessary for Pilate to write the inscription in Greek. In these days French is often called the passport language of the world. But much more than French now was Greek in our Saviour's lifetime on earth such a passport language. It was spoken by all educated persons east of Italy, and we may almost say that it was taught to all well-educated persons in Italy itself, and even in the western states subject to Rome. We do not doubt that Pilate knew and spoke it well; for so prudent an emperor as Tiberius would not have sent to the government of a difficult frontier province like Judæa a man who was not highly cultivated as well as very able.

And all well-educated Jews, we doubt not, knew Greek; they could not help doing so, surrounded as they were by so many to whom it was a current speech.

Whether our blessed Lord, in His daily intercourse with the population of Galilee, used Greek or Aramaic, is a much-disputed question, which cannot, I fear, be settled beyond doubt. There seems to be great *a priori* probability, and in the Gospels themselves there are several well-known indications pointing to the fact, that He familiarly spoke in the Chaldaic Hebrew dialect. But one of our revising company, Professor Roberts, has written a learned book in favour of the other hypothesis, that Greek was the language used by Jesus.

All Jews who sought to become learned men studied Hebrew literature and law under the guidance of some eminent Rabbi. Such was the training of Saul, afterwards Paul, who sat at the feet of Gamaliel. As to the disciples of our blessed Lord, called by Him from the humbler walks of life, we must ascribe their culture as well as the grace they received to His teaching, His society and example, and the influence of that Holy Spirit which furnished them with the intellectual as well as the moral powers essential to their usefulness in the apostolic office. The choice of Greek under that influence for the vehicle of their preaching, their epistles, their historic narratives, is a fact due to the prevalence of that language, as well as to its special excellence. But the Greek of the New Testament is not the subtle, refined, many-stringed instrument of speech, to which the great thinkers of Athens, historians, philosophers, orators, dramatists, attuned the wondrous music of their thought. Its style, especially the style of the four Gospels, is much simpler and homelier, so to say, than that of a Plato, a Demosthenes, or even of a Xenophon. The grandeur of these sacred books is not to be found in the region of high-wrought human language, but in that of divine truth taught to mankind in simple words. New Testament Greek is called Hellenistic—like that of the Septuagint translation and the Apocryphal books.

It is, indeed, a very ancient and by no means improbable tradition that St. Matthew's Gospel was originally written in Aramaic Hebrew, and afterwards translated into Greek either by himself or by another hand. This question is of little concern to our present subject; for as the Hebrew document (if there was such) is lost, and the Greek alone remains to us, scholars have to deal with it as Greek, like all the other books of the New Testament.

The criticism of N. T. Greek is therefore a peculiar work, different in some degree from that of the writings called classical. It requires special reading and acquirement, which are among the studies of young divines in training to become teachers of religious truth to congregations or to pupils.

II. Prominent—perhaps foremost—among the subjects which the young divine has to study with minute care, is the constitution of the Greek text of the New Testament. Can anything be of more momentous importance to Christian people than that they should read the words of our divine Saviour, with the story of His life and actions on earth, as the four Evangelists recorded them, without omission of anything genuine, without intrusion of anything spurious, without departure from the very forms of language in which they wrote? Is it not of like importance that we should read the Acts of our Lord's Apostles exactly as St. Luke has depicted them? that we should learn the doctrine of some—Paul, Peter, James, John, and Jude—in the precise words they used when writing their epistles to Christian churches, or to Christian people generally? or can we have a chance of interpreting aright the darkly foretold future of the book of Revelation, unless we know the precise terms in which its prophetic author wrote?

Thus we see forced upon us the very delicate and disputable question of the genuine text of the New Testament. With this question all students, all translators, all revisers, of that sacred volume are at once brought face to face. Deal with it they must; and they ought to pray earnestly and strive faithfully that they may be enabled to deal with it wisely and well.

You all know that, although 1,880 years and more have passed away since our Saviour's birth, the art of printing books is not yet four centuries and a half old. Before the middle of the fifteenth century all books were in manuscript, written by the human hand on various materials, as parchment, vellum, or paper. The persons employed in copying books of this kind, who, in pagan times, were slaves trained for the duty, were called by the Greeks 'grapheis' or scribes, by the Romans 'librarii,' book-men, or book-makers. In Christian times the copying of books was chiefly carried on by monks or others employed in monasteries. It will easily be supposed that such scribes, like printers who have taken their place, were liable to make mistakes in the performance of their work. And these errors would be of many various kinds, some arising from oversight or carelessness, others from misjudgment. Errors of the former kind are such as misspelling words, mistaking one word for another, dropping out words, going on from a wrong place and so omitting something, and the like. Errors of judgment are still more mischievous. It was a frequent practice of students, old as well as young, to write, in the margin of a manuscript or even within it, words suggesting changes which the writer regarded as just corrections or as improvements; and a scribe copying such a manuscript might adopt any such change, either as approving it honestly, or as considering himself bound in deference to keep it. Such a correction was called 'glossēma,' a gloss; and of these glosses there are numerous examples in the manuscripts of the New Testament. Changes of this kind sometimes arose from a desire to harmonise one place of Holy Writ with another. Thus passages from St. Mark or St. Luke have been intruded into St. Matthew. Sometimes commentators have been tempted to introduce improvements due to their own fancy. Thus the Authorised Version has in Matt. v. 22, 'Whoever is angry with his brother without a cause;' but, as there is no good authority for the words 'without a cause,' the revisers have omitted them. In Matt. vi. the Authorised Version gives three times 'Thy Father which seeth in secret shall reward thee openly.' Again the revisers have omitted the word 'openly,' as being without authority. Differences between manuscripts are called 'various readings:' thus in Matt. ii. 11 some manuscripts have 'they found the child,' but others of greater weight have 'they saw the child,' as in our Bibles; and we say 'they saw' is a better reading than 'they found.' In Matt. xi. 19 the Authorised Version gives 'wisdom is justified of her children;' but the revisers, from the best manuscripts, 'wisdom is justified by her works;' and we had no doubt that the error was that of some harmonising critic who wished to assimilate the place in Matthew to that in Luke vii. 35, where the reading is 'of her children.' But I must leave this part of my subject here.

You see, then, that we are chiefly dependent on manuscripts for textual criticism, and it stands to reason that the oldest are on many grounds the most trustworthy. Until the tenth century, the characters in which scribes wrote were what we now call capitals, but in textual science they are called uncial letters. About the tenth century began a style of writing in small letters, like our handwriting; this style is called cursive. And thus the extant manuscripts are divided into uncial and cursive. Of uncial fewer than a hundred are known, and many of these are fragmentary. Of cursive nearly one thousand are extant. Those which comprise the whole New Testament are few in number compared with those which contain only particular books or fragments. Uncial manuscripts are distinguished from cursive by capital initial letters. The two oldest manuscripts, both of the uncial class, of course, and both of the fourth century, are Codex B in the Vatican Library at Rome, and Codex Sinaiticus, called Aleph, brought from the East in 1859 by Tischendorf, and now in the Library of St. Petersburg. Next to these stand the Codex Alexandrinus (A), in the British Museum; Codex Ephraemi (C), in the National Library at Paris; and Codex Bezæ (D), in the University Library of Cambridge. Next to codices, the most important authorities for the constitution of the text are the ancient versions of the New Testament in various languages.

We find also some assistance in the passages of Scripture cited by Christian writers of the earliest ages, especially by those who are usually called Fathers of the Church.

Finally, we have lectionaries or service-books of the Greek Church, in which the portions of Scripture publicly read throughout the year are set down in chronological order, like the Epistles and Gospels of our Prayer Book. Some of these are uncial, though none perhaps (says Dr. Scrivener) older than the eighth century.

From all these sources useful assistance is obtainable by diligent collation. [*See* Professor E. Abbott's paper, Appendix II.]

With the leading rules and general history of textual criticism all well-read divines are, as a matter of course, more or less familiar. But few can be deemed, few would deem themselves, to be in a special manner masters of the subject, and authorities concerning it, unless they had acquired a practical knowledge of its facts and niceties by the exercise of editorial work. Nor, again, would those scholars who had edited certain portions of the New Testament have been likely to gain so wide and so intimate a knowledge of this large criticism, as those who had devoted many years of life to the formation of a pure text of the whole collection. In the revising company there were several eminent divines who had ably edited various portions of the whole; but three only (since the lamented death of Dean Alford) who had for many years been occupied with the constitution of the entire text; and to these three we naturally and justly looked for the large and definite information which should guide our judgment as to reception or rejection of any disputed reading. Of these divines I first mention the eldest, Dr. Scrivener, to whom, for his editions of the text, his fac-simile editions of codices, and not less for his copious 'Introduction to the Criticism of the New Testament,' Biblical learning owes a deep debt of gratitude. The two others were the Cambridge Professors, Canon Westcott and Dr. Hort, who have for more than twenty years been jointly engaged upon a new edition of the whole text, which is now published, with a second volume containing the valuable introduction and appendix explanatory of the principles and procedure adopted by these excellent scholars. They kindly handed to their colleagues their text of the several portions as our work went on; and the assistance thus supplied was indeed invaluable. Archdeacon Palmer has printed at the Clarendon Press the text which underlies the revised version; and Dr. Scrivener at Cambridge has published the text supposed to have been adopted by the translators of 1611. If capable readers compare these books by the light of the learned and copious volume which I have before cited, Dr. Scrivener's 'Introduction' (second edition, 1874), and now of their own second volume by Westcott and Hort, they will understand why the revision of the text was a work urgently required in the interest of religious truth. In the first place, the translators of 1611 did not possess one tithe of the materials of Biblical criticism which are now accessible to scholars and divines. Especially they knew nothing of those two codices, the most ancient of all, which avail to enlighten us on so many crucial passages, Codex B and Codex Aleph. In the next place, the knowledge of the Greek language itself has been greatly enlarged and improved in this country since the reign of James I.

In these books young students have a body of divinity which, if diligently used, will enable them to form a correct view of all important textual questions affecting the New Testament. We found it very advantageous to our work in the Jerusalem Chamber that the three divines whom I have named represented two somewhat different schools of feeling on that subject. Dr. Scrivener was evidently, I may venture to say avowedly, desirous to show as much favour as he reasonably could to the readings accepted in 1611. So far as I am entitled to state the impression derived from my own observation, I think the judgment of Professors Westcott and Hort was generally determined by the preponderant concurrence of the oldest manuscripts, subject to such control as peculiar conditions might exercise in a few excepted cases. On one conclusion all three critics were assuredly of the same mind, namely, that the value of any reading is to be decided by the weight, not by the number, of the documents which contain it. The agreement of three of the oldest uncial manuscripts in any reading might outweigh the appearance of a different reading in a hundred cursives ; critical skill having shown that these are divisible into families, each traceable to some common original devoid, perhaps, of ancient authority.

The various readings of the Greek New Testament are, as might be expected, very different in their degree of importance. Some of them may be said to have no importance at all in point of sense. Thus it can make no difference whether St. Matthew wrote in chap. ii. that the wise men 'went into the house and *found* the child,' or 'went into the house and *saw* the child,' though the latter reading has the better authority; but whether he wrote in chap. i. of the Virgin Mary, 'till she had brought forth her firstborn son,' as in the Authorised Version, or 'till she had brought forth a son,' as in the revised Testament, makes some small difference, because it is denied by many, as by the Church of Rome, that the mother of Jesus ever bore a second child.

III. Time forbids me to illustrate my subject by citing many of the more important new readings of the revised Testament, but I shall conclude with the mention of four places, in regard to two of which we are acknowledged now by all reasonable divines to be certainly right, while the two others are disputed.

First: the 7th verse of the fifth chapter in St. John's first epistle is thus read in the Authorised Version: 'For there are three that bear record in heaven, the Father, the Word, and the Holy Ghost: and these three are one.' But all that follows the word 'record' is omitted by the revisers; and, although this verse was for many years the subject of voluminous controversy, Dr. Scrivener says with truth that 'to maintain the genuineness of this passage is simply impossible.'

Second: in 1 Tim. iii. 16, where the Authorised Version has 'God was manifest in the flesh,' the revisers write, 'Who was manifest in the flesh.' As I cannot attempt to state the grounds of criticism in a sermon, I will merely say that the decision of the revisers has been anticipated by many divines, as Griesbach, Lachmann, Dean Alford, Bishop Ellicott, and finally by two of our most conservative theologians, Bishop Wordsworth of Lincoln, and Dr. Scrivener.

Third: Matt. vi. 13. All our previous Bibles keep the doxology, 'For Thine is the kingdom, and the power, and the glory, for ever and ever. Amen.' The revisers have cast this into the margin. They have with them

E

Lachmann, Tischendorf, Tregelles, Westcott, and Hort; but here they cannot count Dr. Scrivener among their supporters. He says, 'I am not yet absolutely convinced of its spuriousness.' And at the close of his discussion concerning it, he expresses his opinion that 'the indictment against the last clause of the Lord's Prayer is hitherto unproven.' He says, however, 'It is vain to dissemble the pressure of the adverse case.' Vain indeed, when it is absent from the four earliest extant uncials, Aleph, B, D, Z, from the Latin versions, and the oldest Fathers who expound the Lord's Prayer. It seems to have been unknown in the Western Church, and the impression left on my own mind by consideration of all the evidence is, that the doxology is not a part of the Lord's Prayer as recorded by St. Matthew, but that it was early added by Eastern churches as a good conclusion in liturgies, and so gradually found its way into Eastern Greek Testaments, and thence to a host of cursive manuscripts. This is not to be called an indictment against it, for it is a very good doxology, sound doctrine taken from Chron. xxix. 11, 12; and, as such, it may be retained without objection in our Prayer Book, for it teaches nothing questionable, and was brought in for no party purpose, like the spurious 1 John v. 7.

Fourth : the last twelve verses in St. Mark's Gospel (9–20) are exposed to a suspicion of spuriousness, founded on strong external evidence, and, as some think, further strengthened by their internal character. They have been strenuously defended by Dean Burgon in a very able special treatise; and Dr. Scrivener concurs with him in asserting their genuineness. The revisers have not expunged them, but they leave a break after verse 9, and state the facts concerning this passage in the margin. My own impression hence derived is, that the verses could not be safely quoted in support of any peculiar doctrine, seeing that their authority can always be disputed, as being doubtful.

I now conclude this discourse with the prayer which Dr. Scrivener appends to his instructive volume :

'God grant that, if these studies shall have made any of us better instructed in the letter of the Holy Word, we may find grace to grow, in like measure, in that knowledge which tendeth to salvation, through faith in His mercy by Christ Jesus.'[1]

[1] See Appendix II. A.

SERMON III.

THE REVISED VERSION.

St. John's Gospel v. 39.
Search the Scriptures.

I. So we read in the Authorised Version, but wrongly; the Revised Version writes with just correctness, 'Ye search the Scriptures.' This is manifestly shown to be right by the next words, 'because ye think that in them ye have eternal life.' The doctrine of a future state of rewards and punishments was in those times taught by the Pharisees and their party, who were followed as orthodox by the Jewish people generally; while the Sadducees, who denied this doctrine, were a smaller sect. The teachers of the law naturally sought support for these truths in the Hebrew Scriptures, and they would find in the Psalms and elsewhere texts adapted to their purpose; as in Job xix., 'I know that my Redeemer liveth;' and in Dan. xii.,

'Many of them that sleep in the dust of the earth shall awake, some to everlasting life, and some to shame and everlasting contempt.' To prove this favourite doctrine, says our Lord to the Jews, 'ye search the Scriptures:' then He continues, 'and these are they that bear witness of Me. And ye will not come to Me, that ye may have life.' His argument is, 'Although ye Jews search your own Scriptures diligently, to find in them proofs of a future state of life eternal, yet ye do not find in them, because ye do not search diligently and faithfully, those many texts which bear witness of Me, that I am the Christ, the Son of God, your expected Messiah; and therefore ye do not come to Me that ye may have what ye so much desire— life—life eternal: ye do not come to Me, who am indeed the way, the truth, and the life.'

Thus the verb 'search' in this place is not imperative, but indicative, 'Ye search:' and it is probable that the translators of 1611 chose the wrong form because it gave a useful weapon against the practice of the Church of Rome so far as this was supposed to forbid or condemn the study of Holy Scripture by the laity. There is, however, no lack of texts in our Bible showing that our Lord and His apostles did recommend to all, by precept as well as by example, the diligent study of God's written Word.

II. In my second sermon the correction of the Greek text was the topic specially considered. The necessity of this work was great and urgent. At the same time with the Revised Version appeared two most important books. At Oxford was published the Greek text recognised and adopted by the revising company, at the foot of which are shown the readings apparently received by the translators of 1611, but rejected by the revisers. Conversely, at Cambridge was published the Greek text supposed to have been accepted by the companies of 1611, while at the foot are shown the corrections of that text accepted by the revisers, and also those preferred by some in the revised margin. The variations between the (supposed) text of 1611 and that of 1881, as recorded in these books, exceed five thousand in number. But many of these changes do not affect the English translation at all, and many others, which do affect it, while in a greater or less degree they vary the form of language, leave the real sense of the passage unimpaired. Hence it must be observed that the gravely important varieties of text, though by no means inconsiderable, are but a moderate fraction of the total number recorded in the volumes edited by Archdeacon Palmer and Dr. Scrivener respectively.

At this point I will cite the paragraph in the preface to the Revised Version which deals with the question of text.

'With regard to the Greek text, it would appear that, if to some extent the translators exercised an independent judgment, it was mainly in choosing amongst readings contained in the principal editions of the Greek text that had appeared in the sixteenth century. Wherever they seem to have followed a reading which is not found in any of those editions, their rendering may probably be traced to the Latin Vulgate. Their chief guides appear to have been the later editions of Stephanus and of Beza, and also, to a certain extent, the Complutensian Polyglot. All these were founded for the most part on manuscripts of late date, few in number, and used with little critical skill. But in those days it could hardly have been otherwise. Nearly all the more ancient of the documentary authorities have become known only within the last two centuries; some of the most important of them, indeed, within the last few years. Their publication has called forth not only improved editions of the Greek text, but a succession of instructive discussions on the variations which have been brought to light, and on the best modes of distinguishing original readings from changes introduced in the course of transcription. While, therefore, it has long been the opinion of all scholars that the commonly received text needed thorough revision, it is but recently that materials have been acquired for executing such a work with even approximate completeness.'

This passage refers to the textual question in a general and cursory manner only. It was beyond the scope of a preface to do more than this; any detailed account would have required a volume such as Dr. Scrivener's 'Introduction,' noticed in a former sermon: or such as that second appendix now gained from the labours of Canon Westcott and Dr. Hort, besides which appendix, the pages (541–562) subjoined to their first volume deserve the studious attention of all theologians, clerical or lay, forming as they do a comprehensive outline of facts and principles applicable to the textual criticism and constitution of the New Testament.

Leaving now the question of the Greek text,

I propose in this discourse to speak of variant English renderings in places where the original is either undisputed, or only partially questioned. But in so vast a field as this it is evident that my exemplification must be limited to a few instances of peculiar interest and importance.

Here, again, it suits my purpose to cite the modest language of the preface to the Revised Version.

'We know full well that defects must have their place in a work so long and so arduous as this which has now come to an end. Blemishes and imperfections there are in the noble translation which we have been called upon to revise; blemishes and imperfections will assuredly be found in our own revision. All endeavours to translate the Holy Scriptures into another tongue must fall short of their aim, when the obligation is imposed of producing a version that shall be alike literal and idiomatic, faithful to each thought of the original, and yet, in the expression of it, harmonious and free. While we dare to hope that in places not a few of the New Testament the introduction of slight changes has cast a new light upon much that was difficult and obscure, we cannot forget how often we have failed in expressing some finer shade of meaning which we recognised in the original, how often idiom has stood in the way of a perfect rendering, and how often the attempt to preserve a familiar form of words, or even a familiar cadence, has only added another perplexity to those which already beset us.'

Yes, the existence of blemishes in the revised volume, thus acknowledged by the collective voice of the company, would certainly not be denied by any individual member; yet if we were severally required to furnish lists of what we regard as blemishes, it is more than probable that no two lists would exactly coincide.

Some would, perhaps, allow that the language of the Authorised Version has occasionally been altered without adequate reason, and with no real improvement; as when we write, 'Thy will be done, as in heaven, so on earth,' for the usual rendering, 'Thy will be done in earth, as it is in heaven.' Others would endorse a complaint very commonly made, that the Greek connective particles are too scrupulously represented in our translation, to the detriment of English idiom as well as of melodious rhythm. They might note many examples illustrating this opinion in the Synoptic Gospels; for instance, in chapters viii., ix., xiii., xiv. of St. Matthew. The American critics would find in the minority of the company support for some of their views, as printed at the close of the Revised Version. But in these cases, and in others which could be suggested, it may be that the decision of the majority, for which strong reasons were always urged, was wiser than the judgment of those who voted in a contrary sense; and if it were not always so, yet a few such errors or shortcomings are not a feather in the scale when weighed against the vast improvements wrought in the textual constitution of the Greek, and the verbal expression of the English New Testament, by the labours now brought to a conclusion, which I would fain hope is not unalterably permanent.

But I must digress no further from the special subject of this day's consideration—the English renderings of undisputed Greek words.

III. One new rendering in the revision has been received with general but not universal favour. I allude to the well-known passage, Acts xxvi. 28, which in the Authorised Version is, 'Then Agrippa said unto Paul, Almost thou persuadest me to be a Christian.' We have a question of reading here as well as of interpretation. The translators of 1611 found a verb which they render 'to be,' though they ought to have written it 'to become' a Christian. But the revisers, from the three oldest uncials, and several versions, have received a different verb, 'to make,' and they write the words, 'with but little persuasion thou wouldst fain make me a Christian.' This is a good rendering, and assuredly a true one. Literally the words are, 'in a little thou usest persuasion to make me a Christian.' The idiomatic phrase 'in a little' may imply 'space of time' or 'number of words,' which amount to the same thing here; and king Agrippa in effect says, 'You are such an enthusiast, O Paul, that you think it will take little time and few words to make me a Christian.' Yet this excellent interpretation is said to be contested by no less a person than Dr. Ryle, Bishop of Liverpool. His words, reported in *Public Opinion* by a hearer of his sermon, are the following:—" I hold with Luther, Beza, Grotius, Poole, Bengel, and Stier, that the translation given in our Authorised Version is right and correct. I am fortified in my belief by the fact that this is the view of one who thought and spoke and wrote in the language of the New Testament; I mean the famous Greek

Father Chrysostom. And last, but not least, no other view appears to me to harmonise with the exclamation of the apostle St. Paul in the verse which follows : 'Almost,' he seems to say, taking up Agrippa's words; ' I want thee to be not almost, but altogether a Christian."—Now, without weighing opinion against opinion (though I could cite crowds of eminent scholars and divines who differ from the Bishop and those whom he cites), I must declare my entire conviction that the authorised rendering is untenable on every ground which can be specified : first, because the true reading is '*to make,*' not '*to be*' or '*to become*;' secondly, because 'almost' is an incorrect rendering of the Greek phrase; thirdly, because the verb does not in good Greek prose mean 'thou persuadest' in the Bishop's sense, but 'thou-art-using-persuasion ;' fourthly, because ' Christianos,' a Christian, was at that time a term of opprobrium or contempt ; and St. Paul does not say in his reply, ' I wish thou and all who hear me this day might become Christians,' but ' I wish ye might become such as I am, except these bonds.' Agrippa uses the sneering appellation 'Christianon.' Paul does not embrace it as a glorious name ; no, he only says 'such as I am,' with the courteous exception of his chains. Neither Paul nor any of the apostles ever call themselves Christians. St. Luke tells us that the disciples were first so called at Antioch; yes, so called they were in contemptuous reproach. Hence St. Peter says in his first epistle, iv. 16, 'If a man suffer as a Christian, let him not be *ashamed*, but let him glorify God *in this name.*' Even so the Christians of the Reformation 350 years ago were contemptuously called Protestants on account of the protest made against an edict of the Diet of Speier; but the martyrs of Mary's reign in England were not *ashamed* to suffer under the name of Protestants, protesting, as they deemed, against false doctrine and mischievous superstition.

While, however, I am sure that the 'almost and altogether' of the Authorised Version is totally wrong, I am not quite satisfied with the revised rendering of verse 29. I regret that the 'would to God' of the Authorised Version has been kept. I believe (with Webster and Wilkinson) the right translation to be this: 'I would pray to God, whether with little prayer or with much, that not thou only, but also all that hear me this day, might become such as I am, except these bonds.'

When Bishop Ryle has reconsidered the authoritative reading, and the just sense of the several words, I venture to believe that he will abandon the old error here.

IV. The revisers are blamed, to my great surprise, by some high authorities, such as the *Times* and the *Edinburgh Review*, because in 1 Cor. xiii., and everywhere else, they have (with Tyndale) rendered the Greek word 'agăpē' by the English 'love,' instead of retaining the word 'charity,' which the translators of 1611 unhappily imported from the 'caritas' of Jerome's Latin version, known as the Vulgate, or perhaps from its daughter, the Rhemish version. I venture to affirm that, as scholars, having a just regard for the proprieties of language, it was impossible for us to adopt any other rendering than love (to love), as Luther and other German translators have 'liebe' (lieben), and nothing else. I must put the question before you with some fulness of detail.

The Greek language has various words meaning 'love' and 'to love.' 'Philos' is 'a friend;' 'philein,' to love in a friendly way; 'philia,' friendship. 'Storgē' is a word of somewhat rare use, the love of kin, mainly that of parents for their offspring; the verb being 'stergein.' 'Erōs,' with its verb 'erân,' expresses love as a passion, not only sexually, but in all metaphors of an analogous nature, as love of pleasure, love of money, love of power, and the like. Lastly, we have the beautiful noun 'agăpē,' with its verb 'agapân,' which may be used, and is in Scripture used, for all or any of these feelings when they are pure and lovely and of good report. Let me exemplify its use in a few texts:—(1) As to earthly feeling and conduct: Eph. v. 25, 'Husbands, love your wives,' with all that follows. Love of our brother, love of the saints, are again and again so recommended. Gal. v. 13, 'By love serve one another.' But need I do more than read to you that passage of St. Paul, Rom. xiii. 8, 9, 10?—'Owe no man any thing, but to love one another: for he that loveth his neighbour hath fulfilled the law. Every commandment is summed up in this word, namely, Thou shalt love thy neighbour as thyself. Love worketh no ill to his neighbour: love therefore is the fulfilment of the law.' Such is agapân, such is agăpē, between man and man. What need we else? Why import the Latin 'caritas,' charity, to supersede the sweet Teutonic word 'liebe' (love) in 1 Cor. xiii., and a few other places, as our former translators have unfortunately done? (2) But the use of these excellent words in Scripture is not confined to earthly relations. They are used in Holy Writ to express what the Divine Being feels towards His rational creatures, what His rational creatures ought to feel towards Him. The love of God, the love of Christ, are set forth in both senses, as our duty and as our blessing; and the whole is crowned by the wondrously thrilling, the deeply comforting assurance of the beloved disciple St. John, that 'God is love.' And all this is declared to us by the word agăpē.

It remains to ask how it was that Jerome thought proper to render that word by 'caritas,' and why (if indeed we can find any reason) our own translators adopted it partially in the form 'charity.' Jerome's reason is perhaps not far to seek. For 'love' the Latin language has but one comprehensive word, 'amor;' its verb being 'amare,' to love. But there is a second verb, 'diligere,' properly meaning to choose, but also used in the sense which we often express by the word 'liking,' or even mildly 'loving;' and from this verb a noun was coined and

F

sometimes used in later Latin, 'dilectio,' whence we get the word 'predilection.'

The words 'amor,' 'amare,' are used to express all kinds of earthly love, good or not. Divine love in any pure and lofty sense was not known to the heathen world in general, only perhaps to a few philosophers. Owing to the frequent abuse of those words by some licentious Latin writers, Jerome was, we think, unwilling to apply them to the pure and virtuous love of Christian brethren, or to the high and holy love which links the creature with the Creator, the redeemed with the Redeemer. Hence he adopted instead of 'amor' another classical word, distorting its sense, and applying it too largely. I mean the word 'caritas.' You know that 'carus' (Ital. *caro*, French *cher*) means in English 'dear,' and its substantive 'caritas' means therefore 'dearness,' and has properly an objective sense only, that character or quality which causes some person or thing to be dear. Thus a Roman would say, 'My country attaches me to itself by a strong dearness;' or two friends might be said to be united by a mutual dearness, and the like. This noun, I say, Jerome, avoiding 'amor,' thought proper to misuse by adopting it in all the senses, subjective and objective, which 'amor' can assume. He has therefore used it throughout the whole of his Latin translation (the Vulgate), even in St. John's epistles and other places, where the love of God and of Christ are set forth. He has not shrunk even from writing 'Deus est caritas,' God is carity (charity).

But what was he to do for a verb? If he used 'caritas,' dearness, for 'amor,' love, he could not say 'caritare to charity,' for 'amare to love,' seeing that 'caritas' is objective in its proper use, and has no verb of its own. What then did Jerome do? He took the lukewarm word 'diligere,' 'to choose with a liking,' 'to like,' and so 'to love.' And this verb he has used for 'amare' in almost all the places where the Greek has agăpân. Fancy 'Love thy neighbour as thyself' in this shape, 'Choose thy neighbour with a liking as thou choosest thyself;' or, for 'Christ loved us,' 'Christ chose us with a liking,' and gave Himself for us! At such disadvantage has Jerome placed the whole theory and practice of holy Christian love in his Latin version of the New Testament. Meaning, no doubt, to do right, he did wrong; meaning to do good, he did harm. And why, again and again I ask, why did the translators of 1611 adopt his degenerate word 'caritas' in 1 Cor. xiii., and in some twenty other places which Cruden's 'Concordance' will show you, when they shrank from adopting it throughout the first two Epistles of St. John, and in some seventy places besides, and when they have rendered agăpân by the English verb 'to love' everywhere? Here they were hampered. They had no such refuge as Jerome's 'diligere,' poor as that is; 'to like' was impossible; the beautiful word 'lichen,' to love, stood alone, they could not do other than take it. Why then their 'charity'? I cannot be sure. I can only guess. I imagine that in 1 Cor. xiii. they wished for a noun which should be free from any tinge or suspicion of passionateness, and so they laid hold on Jerome's 'caritas,' which the Rhemish version would give as 'charity,' and sprinkled the same word here and there 'charily' to give it more vogue. Their motive we may not doubt was good, but their reasoning and their conclusion were bad, and the revisers of 1881 could not possibly avoid reversing their decision.

But some will say, with counter-protest, the Authorised Version has given to this word 'charity' a home in our language, and we cannot

do without it : is it to disappear from our Bibles ?
is its very foundation to be removed ? are we to
lose it ? To this last question I answer at once,
No. The English language has got the word
'charity,' and that word it will keep, though
'love' be read in 1 Cor. xiii. The revisers
as little had the will as they had the power to
expunge a word from our dictionaries, to deny
it a place in our literature, to forbid its use in
daily conversation. The word 'charity' has
nothing to fear from ceasing to stand in the
epistles of Scripture. But, let me ask, has
English usage preserved that high ideal of
Christian love of one's neighbour which St.
Paul depicts in that beautiful chapter ? Surely
not. Charity, in common parlance, has these
meanings : (1) beneficence, a beneficent act, or a
beneficent institution ; (2) that disposition or
principle of thought and conduct which leads us
to think and speak as little evil and as much good
of others as we possibly can. And the epithet
'charitable' we apply in these senses : (1) beneficent, (2) putting the best construction on
the acts and characters of others. But do
these definitions exhaust St. Paul's description
of Christian 'agăpē'? No. Beneficence is
expressly distinguished from 'agăpē' in v. 3 :

Bestowing goods profiteth nothing without love. And yet I venture to say that the word 'charity' is used more than twenty times by English folk and in English writings as referring to beneficence, for once that it is used in that second signification, which comes nearer to the picture of love, as 'being kind,' as taking no account of evil, as 'rejoicing not in unrighteousness,' as 'believing all things, hoping all things.' Yet even these features do not complete the portrait of Christian 'agăpē.' Finally, then, I repeat, that the revisers have most assuredly done right in replacing everywhere (for 'agăpē') the Latin word 'charity' by that Saxon word 'love,' which the Authorised Version itself uses in seventy passages instead of Jerome's word; while the cognate verb 'to love,' in that version as well as in the revised, is employed throughout the New Testament. Against these facts, and the conclusion to which they point, can any weighty argument be found?

V. There is, I suppose, no feature in the Revised Version which has been more assailed by the outside world than its mode of dealing with the Lord's Prayer. I must therefore not conclude this sermon without endeavouring to quiet any alarm you may have felt respecting it.

The prayer as read in the eleventh chapter of St. Luke, 1-4, is, by the authority of manuscripts, reduced to the following words:

'Father, hallowed be Thy name. Thy kingdom come. Give us day by day our daily bread. And forgive us our sins; for we ourselves also forgive every one that is indebted to us. And bring us not into temptation.'

In St. Matthew vi. 9-13 the revisers depart from the Authorised by writing,—

(1) 'Thy will be done, as in heaven, so on earth.'

To many this inversion, though literal, seems unnecessary.

(2) 'Have forgiven' in the place of 'forgive.'

This is required by a new reading.

(3) 'And bring us not into temptation.'

This change is right, because the Greek in both Gospels means 'bring,' and because 'lead' is an over-strong and painful word drawn from the Vulgate, and used there for the reason that Latin has no verb which adequately represents 'bring' in the sense required here.

(4) 'But deliver us from the evil one.'

The revisers are, as might be expected, severely censured for writing 'the evil one,' where the Greek would equally well bear the Authorised rendering 'evil.' Let me say that the majority who voted this change included excellent scholars and divines of high repute. Their arguments were exceedingly strong, and not easy to confute. But a minority still doubt whether the alteration is worth keeping in the face of wide dissatisfaction, and whether the protest of a margin ought not to content those who strongly believe in the concrete sense of the Greek term used by our Lord here.[1]

Remember this one thing, my Christian brethren, that, if the Revised Testament were authorised for public use at once, it would not follow that any change need be made in the Lord's Prayer as it now stands in our Common Prayer Book and in the Church Catechism. For at the present time the forms used in our

[1] In *Public Opinion* I find a provincial journalist cited as saying that in future times the revisers of 1881 will be known as those who introduced the devil into the Lord's Prayer. I would invite his attention to Matt. iv. 1-11; xiii. 19, 38, 39; Luke x. 17, 18; Acts xxvi. 15-18; 1 John iii. 8; v. 18, 19. In the same *Public Opinion* I read, in a letter of Mr. Dykes: 'Of the many beauties of the Revised Version I reckon none more acceptable than the changed ending of Matt. vi. 13, having long sympathised with the complaint of good John Berridge of Everton, in his 'Christian World Unmasked,' that whereas the devil's name was originally in the Lord's Prayer, 'some roguish body' had wiped it out.

Church Services do not exactly agree with those which appear in the Authorised Versions of St. Matthew and St. Luke. We do not say 'forgive us our debts' with St. Matthew, nor 'forgive us our sins' with St. Luke. And we may still repeat the ascription of glory at the close, even though we deem it to have been added with the best intentions by pious Eastern bishops.

These considerations should set every mind at ease about this cherished form of prayer, and assist us now in ascribing to God, the Father, Son, and Holy Spirit, 'the kingdom and the power and the glory for ever and ever. Amen.'[1]

[1] Appendix III. shows all the places of real importance in which the Revised Version differs from the Authorised.

APPENDICES.

APPENDIX I.

I THINK it right to append a few words in defence of some interpretations of passages in the New Testament as adopted in Sermon I.

I. 1 Cor. ii. 13, πνευματικὰ πνευματικοῖς συγκρίνοντες. Here the Authorised Version renders 'comparing spiritual things with spiritual;' and this is kept in the Revised Version. I have declared my conviction that the competing translation, 'explaining spiritual things to spiritual men,' which stands in our margin, is the right one. Biblical scholars do not deny that the verb συγκρίνω can have this sense in Hellenistic Greek, though the usage is not classical. In my view, explained by my paraphrase, the logic of the whole context demands that πνευματικοῖς should be taken as masculine (to spiritual men), not as neuter (spiritual things). (1) St. Paul immediately goes on to say: 'The psychic [*i.e.* the merely intellectual] man cannot receive spiritual things, but the spiritual man judgeth all things, and he is not subject to the judgment of the psychic man. But to you Corinthians, unhappily, I could not speak as to spiritual men, seeing that you are carnal.' All this consecution refers to πνευματικοῖς, spiritual men, in v. 13. Nor does it seem unimportant that the verb κρίνει thus speedily follows its compound συγκρίνει. The help in judging which one spiritual man gives another has for its result, that each κρίνει, is able to judge. (2) The whole chapter dwells not upon inspired writings, but upon inspired men. St. Paul claims for himself and the other apostles that they are such : but their disciples also must be inspired men, πνευματικοὶ (spiritual, not carnal), in order to receive spiritual teaching profitably. Worldly wisdom and worldly greatness avail nothing for such a purpose (vv. 5-9, 14). We apostles, he says (he the only learned one in the ordinary sense), tell you the things bestowed by the grace of God (12, 13) not in words taught of human wisdom, but in words taught of the Holy Spirit, to which he adds, πνευματικὰ πνευματικοῖς συγκρίνοντες. Now if these three words are rendered as in the Authorised Version, and explained, as Prof. Blunt understood them, 'comparing one place of Scripture (*i.e.* the Old Testament) with another,' then we have a purely intellectual (psychic) operation, the work of a scholarly student, rudely thrust in here, and jarring, as a false note, with the whole tone of the chapter, which calls upon 'spiritual men' to accept, as its proper recipients, 'the spiritual teaching' of the inspired fishermen of Galilee as well as that of the inspired student of Tarsus. It may be that some persons defend the Authorised Version without narrowing it to the comparison of written documents. I cannot fully estimate any such view without having it before me. Yet it seems to me that it can only consist in some mystical notion of

St. Paul's inner consciousness. And this would seem to me a σοφία not less rudely introduced, not less jarring with the tone of the context, than the more limited sense in which Prof. Blunt has taken the words. I cannot therefore reconcile myself to any interpretation but that which makes πνευματικοῖς masculine. I think it is masculine also in xii. 1, because the immediate context speaks of the distinguishing signs of spiritual men. But as the chapter goes on to treat of spiritual things also, the error, if it be one, is not of much importance.

II. Rom. viii. 33-4. We read in the Authorised Version, 'Who shall lay any thing to the charge of God's elect? *It is* God that justifieth. Who is he that condemneth? *It is* Christ that died, yea rather, that is risen again, who is even at the right hand of God, who also maketh intercession for us.'

This version assumes that full stops are to be placed after 'justifieth' and 'for us;' and that the only notes of interrogation are those which follow the words 'elect' and 'condemneth.' Also it assumes that the true reading is ὁ κατακρίνων, 'he that condemneth,' not ὁ κατακρινῶν, 'he that shall condemn.' Tittmann's edition has (except that it keeps κατακρίνων) Τίς ἐγκαλέσει κατὰ ἐκλεκτῶν Θεοῦ; Θεὸς ὁ δικαιῶν; τίς ὁ κατακρινῶν; Χριστὸς ὁ ἀποθανών; μᾶλλον δὲ καὶ ἐγερθείς; ὃς καὶ ἔστιν ἐν δεξιᾷ τοῦ Θεοῦ; ὃς καὶ ἐντυγχάνει ὑπὲρ ἡμῶν; I think commas would answer the purpose after ἀποθανών, ἐγερθείς, and τοῦ Θεοῦ, but (with this variation) I have no doubt Tittmann is right. The superior force and beauty of the interrogatives can escape no intelligent mind: and what clinches the argument in their favour is the exact parallelism of the next verse, 35: Τίς ἡμᾶς χωρίσει ἀπὸ τῆς ἀγάπης τοῦ Χριστοῦ; θλίψις, ἢ στενοχωρία, ἢ διωγμός, ἢ λιμός, ἢ γυμνότης, ἢ κίνδυνος, ἢ μάχαιρα; Therefore I would render 33, 34, 'Who shall accuse God's elect? Will God who justifieth? Who is he that shall condemn? Will Christ who died, nay more, who also rose, who is also on God's right hand, who also intercedeth for us?' The words 'yea rather,' and 'even,' in the Authorised, are very faulty.

III. Phil. iii. 16, 17. The words of 16, πλὴν, εἰς ὃ ἐφθάσαμεν, τῷ αὐτῷ στοιχεῖν, are much more fitly taken as a modest preface to v. 17 than in the very harsh construction which makes στοιχεῖν an infinitive used imperatively, refers τῷ αὐτῷ to the relative ὅ, and puts a full stop after στοιχεῖν. The words εἰς ὃ ἐφθάσαμεν are a well-known parenthetic idiom—quoniam huc (*i.e.* ad hanc doctrinam) processimus, ut eadem via graderemur; the clause τῷ αὐτῷ στοιχεῖν being in apposition to the relative ὅ. I render, therefore, 'Nevertheless, as we have so far attained, to walk by the same rule, brethren, be ye with common consent imitators of me,' &c.: *i.e.* as we have learnt the duty and wisdom of union and uniform conduct. The context before and after v. 16 proves that it is so connected with v. 17 and what follows.

IV. Rom. ix. 5. On this important passage I have for very many years felt no doubt that the punctuation and interpretation given in my sermon are true. There are four various punctuations, and four corresponding translations, which I will first set down, and then discuss in my own order.

APPENDIX I. 79

(1) καὶ ἐξ ὧν ὁ Χριστὸς τὸ κατὰ σάρκα, ὁ ὢν ἐπὶ πάντων, Θεὸς εὐλογητὸς εἰς τοὺς αἰῶνας· ἀμήν. Auth. Vers. 'and of whom according to the flesh Christ came, who is over all, God blessed for ever. Amen.'

(2) καὶ ἐξ ὧν ὁ Χριστὸς τὸ κατὰ σάρκα. Ὁ ὢν ἐπὶ πάντων Θεὸς εὐλογητὸς εἰς τοὺς αἰῶνας· ἀμήν. 'And of whom is the Christ after the flesh. God who is over all be (is) blessed for ever. Amen.'

(3) καὶ ἐξ ὧν ὁ Χριστὸς τὸ κατὰ σάρκα, ὁ ὢν ἐπὶ πάντων. Θεὸς εὐλογητὸς εἰς τοὺς αἰῶνας· ἀμήν. 'And of whom is the Christ after the flesh, who is over all. God be (is) blessed for ever. Amen.'

(4) καὶ ἐξ ὧν ὁ Χριστὸς τὸ κατὰ σάρκα. Ὁ ὢν ἐπὶ πάντων Θεός, εὐλογητὸς εἰς τοὺς αἰῶνας· ἀμήν. 'And of whom is the Christ after the flesh. He who is over all *is* God, blessed for ever. Amen.'

The last of these is the interpretation which I have advocated as the only true, the only unobjectionable one. I shall now compare it in the first instance with (2) and (3). Each of these latter labours under a weighty objection, which has been constantly urged against them: namely, that in the elliptical ascription of blessing εὐλογητὸς or εὐλογημένος is elsewhere (and ought to be) the first word. From this objection (4) is exempt, for it makes the words ὁ ὢν ἐπὶ πάντων Θεός a sentence, Θεός being its predicative noun, to which εὐλογητὸς belongs as an adjunct epithet. The ellipse of ἐστί in such a sentence is one of the most ordinary character, and indeed almost demanded by the presence of ὤν. The grammatical construction is therefore unimpeachable. A much bolder ellipsis of ἐστί before the predicative Θεὸς appears 2 Cor. i. 21: ὁ δὲ βεβαιῶν ἡμᾶς σὺν ὑμῖν εἰς Χριστὸν καὶ χρίσας ἡμᾶς, Θεός. But θεὸς εὐλογητὸς for θεὸς ἔστω εὐλογητὸς I regard as far from unimpeachable. No example of the ellipse of a third person imperative has ever to my mind been satisfactorily established, though that of opt. εἴη occurs in every epistle. That from this ascription in the New Testament 'be' should be excluded and 'is'. adopted seems proved by Rom. i. 25, ὅς ἐστιν εὐλογητός, with which corresponds 2 Cor. xi. 31, ὁ ὢν εὐλογητός. (In John xii. 13, A. V. writes 'is.') Therefore I hold that in Eph. i. 3, 'Blessed is' should be written for 'Blessed be.' Again in 1 Pet. i. 3. Thus, while doctrinally there is no important distinction between (2) and (4), yet, grammatically, (4) is incomparably superior.

It remains to consider the Authorised Version, which has to encounter objections of a different kind, objections which I hold to be fatal to it. For—

1. While St. Paul distinctly declares our Lord's divine nature in at least two chapters, Phil. ii., Col. i., and, I think, implies it always, there are but two places where he is supposed to ascribe to Him the predicate θεός, while the passages are numerous in which he purposely distinguishes between ὁ θεός (ὁ πατήρ), and ὁ κύριος Ἰησοῦς Χριστός.

To these passages I must now invite attention.

(1) No passage is more important in this discussion than the opening verses of Romans, chap. i., since in these St. Paul treats doctrinally of Christ's nature. Himself is set apart (he says) to carry 'the

good tidings (gospel) of God . . . concerning His Son, —who was born, after His human nature (flesh), of David's lineage ; but after His divine nature (the Spirit of holiness) was declared miraculously (ἐν δυνάμει), by rising from the dead, to be the Son of God—even Jesus Christ our Lord.' In other words, that same Jesus, whom we acknowledge to be Christ the Lord, was declared to be the Son of God (the divine Messiah), not, be it observed, to be Θεὸς ἐπὶ πάντων.

(2) Next let us observe the relation between Θεός (πατήρ) and 'Ιησοῦς Χριστός, as exhibited in the salutations prefixed to the various epistles of St. Paul.

- Rom. i. 7 : χάρις ὑμῖν καὶ εἰρήνη ἀπὸ Θεοῦ πατρὸς ἡμῶν καὶ κυρίου 'Ιησοῦ Χριστοῦ : 'Grace to you and peace from God our Father and the Lord Jesus Christ.'
- The same is found in 1 Cor. i. 3 ; 2 Cor. ii. 2 ; Eph. i. 2 ; Phil. i. 2.
- Gal. i. 2 and 2 Thess. i. 2 have the same, except 'the' for 'our.'
- Col. : 'Grace to you and peace from God our Father,' (followed by) 'We give thanks to God the Father of our Lord Jesus Christ,' &c.
- 1 Thess. i. 1 : 'Unto the church of the Thessalonians in God the Father and the Lord Jesus Christ : Grace to you and peace.'
- 1 Tim. i. 2 : 'Grace, mercy, peace, from God the Father and Christ Jesus our Lord.'
- 2 Tim. i. 2 : As in 1 Tim.

G

Tit. i. 4: 'Grace and peace from God the Father, and Christ Jesus our Saviour.'

(3) The following passages are cited from other parts of St. Paul's epistles:—

Rom. xv. 6: 'That with one accord ye may with one mouth glorify the God and Father of our Lord Jesus Christ.'

1 Cor. i. 9: 'God is faithful, through whom ye were called into the fellowship of His Son Jesus Christ our Lord;' viii. 6: 'To us there is one God, the Father, ... and one Lord Jesus Christ.'

2 Cor. i. 3: 'Blessed *be* [*is*] the God and Father of our Lord Jesus Christ;' repeated Eph. i. 3: 'The Son of God, Jesus Christ.' (*See* also iv. 6; v. 19.)

Gal. i. 1: 'Through Jesus Christ, and God the Father.'

Eph. vi. 23: 'Peace be to the brethren, and love with faith, from God the Father and the Lord Jesus Christ.' (*See* v. 20.)

Phil. ii. 5–11. (This great crucial passage as rendered in Revised Version should be carefully pondered.)

Col. (Chapters i., ii., and iii. to verse 17 are essential to the study of the question before us; they declare Christ's divinity very plainly, but nowhere call Him Θεός.)

1 Thess. iii. 11: 'Now may our God and Father Himself, and our Lord Jesus, direct our way unto you.' (*See* i. 3, 9, 10.)

2 Thess. i. 12: 'That the name of our Lord

APPENDIX I.

Jesus Christ may be glorified in you, and ye in Him, according to the grace of our God and the Lord Jesus Christ;' ii. 16: 'Now our Lord Jesus Christ Himself, and God our Father' &c. (Observe the loftiness of divinity which this verse, and the whole of this early epistle, ascribe to the Lord Jesus Christ, but without calling Him Θεός.)

1 Tim. i. 1: 'Paul, an apostle of Christ Jesus, according to the commandment of God our Saviour, and Christ Jesus our hope.' See in i. 12, &c., the greatness and goodness of 'Christ Jesus our Lord,' the Saviour of sinners and ensample of all that shall believe in Him; ending with the doxology 17: Now unto the King eternal, incorruptible, invisible, the only God, *be* [*is*] honour and glory for ever and ever. Amen. (Compare ii. 5, 6, and the memorable place, iii. 16, which, by the reading ὅς, now universally received, calls Jesus Himself the μυστήριον θεότητος, as in Col. ii. 2, 3.) See v. 21; vi. 13.

2 Tim. iv. 1: 'I charge thee in the sight of God and of Christ Jesus' &c.

Our quotations from St. Paul's epistles have now brought us face to face with the passage, Tit. ii. 13. This is the only place in which I am, unhappily, compelled to argue against the rendering of the Revised Version, except in the passages upon which my opinion was expressed in my sermon of 1861 at Cambridge, now reprinted; it being understood that I was free to defend those opinions. And this defence involves a defence of the Authorised Version in rendering here τοῦ μεγάλου Θεοῦ καὶ Σωτῆρος ἡμῶν Ἰησοῦ Χριστοῦ, 'the great God and our Saviour Jesus Christ.' This the majority of the revisers have placed in the margin, giving in their text 'our great God and Saviour Jesus Christ.' My friend Mr. Humphry, in his tract, p. 10, applauds and welcomes this decision as 'a more clear declaration of the Godhead of Christ.' I am sorry to differ from him, but I do differ from him— I will not say *toto cœlo*, for I think the Scriptural declaration of Christ's Godhead stands in no need of this translation, nor of that received in Rom. ix. 5. To my mind the doctrine is clearly enough declared in Phil. and Col., and assumed by the apostle throughout his writings, as well as in his history given by St. Luke. But I believe that he has everywhere avoided predicating Christ by the title Θεός, and I point to the passage 1 Tim. i. 12–17, crowned by ii. 5–7 and iii. 16, and illustrated by the two epistles above named and by Rom. i., &c., as containing and justifying the view which I take of his doctrinal standpoint on this μυστήριον θεότητος. Its logical completion, as deduced from his writings and those of other apostles and evangelists, came in God's good time at another epoch of Church history. Referring to the Greek of this passage, I admit, of course, the possibility, nay, even the plausibility of the rendering in the revised text. But I do not concede its necessity; and I contest its analogical fitness, as compared with St. Paul's writings generally, and with this epistle itself. Necessary it is not. As a Greek scholar, I deny that σωτῆρος ἡμῶν is necessarily controlled by the article τοῦ before μεγάλου Θεοῦ: and I feel assured that St. Paul, having written in i. 4 'from God the Father and Christ Jesus our Saviour,' would not have expected anybody reading this Greek to doubt that τοῦ μεγάλου Θεοῦ represents Θεοῦ πατρός, and Σωτῆρος ἡμῶν 'Ιησοῦ Χριστοῦ represents the previous Χριστοῦ 'Ιησοῦ τοῦ Σωτῆρος ἡμῶν. If such were the mind of Paul when he wrote this, he might fearlessly omit the second article before Σωτῆρος, as Æschylus has omitted it before κρατησάντων in the passage καὶ τῶν ἁλόντων καὶ κρατησάντων δίχα | φωνὰς ἀκούειν ἔστι, *Agam.* 301. The poet, departing from grammatical usage, omits a second τῶν before κρατησάντων: why? because the captured and the conquerors could not be taken for the same, and his readers or his audience could make no mistake. Neither would St. Paul deem it necessary to place a τοῦ before σωτῆρος, as he had never called Christ Jesus 'the great God,' and in the beginning of his epistle he had called Him 'our Saviour,' distinctly from God the Father. If, indeed, he had written τοῦ Θεοῦ καὶ σωτῆρος, there might have been some chance of mistake;[1] but the epithet μεγάλου removes, or ought to remove, all chance, being a well-known Old Testament attribute of the supreme God. Even in the Revelations, v. 13, to which the passage before us leads attention, we find

[1] Yet in 1 Tim. v. 21 the Auth. renders τοῦ Θεοῦ καὶ Κυρίου 'Ιησοῦ Χριστοῦ, ' God, and the Lord Jesus Christ.' The Revision omits Κυρίου, rendering ' God, and Jesus Christ.'

distinction still kept between God and the glorified Jesus (ch. i.), between 'Him who sitteth on the throne' and 'the Lamb.' On these grounds I hope to be forgiven for saying that I adhere to the Authorised Version of Tit. ii. 13, which now stands in the revised margin; and since (with Mr. Humphry) I do not advocate 'servile adherence to the Greek order,' I should not have been disturbed if 'the Saviour' had ended the verse, as in i. 4. Thus my conclusion is that Tit. ii. 13 can never be justly cited as proving that St. Paul has designated Christ Jesus by the predicate Θεός. Of Rom. ix. 5 I say the same.

Let us now compare the other doxologies found in St. Paul's writings with that in Rom. ix. 5.

> Rom. i. 25 : 'And worshipped and served the creature rather than the Creator, who is blessed for ever. Amen.'
>
> Rom. xi. 36 : 'To Him *be* [*is*] the glory for ever. Amen.'
>
> 2 Cor. xi. 31 : 'The God and Father of the Lord Jesus, He who is blessed for evermore, knoweth that I lie not.'
>
> Gal. i. 5 : 'Our God and Father; to whom *be* [*is*] the glory for ever and ever. Amen.'
>
> Eph. i. 3 : 'Blessed *be* [*is*] the God and Father of our Lord Jesus Christ.' (So 1 Pet. i. 3.)
>
> Eph. iii. 21 : ' Unto Him *be* [*is*] the glory in the church and in Christ Jesus unto all generations for ever and ever. Amen.'
>
> Phil. iv. 20 : 'Now unto God our Father *be* [*is*] the glory for ever and ever. Amen.'
>
> 1 Tim. i. 17 : 'Now unto the King eternal,

APPENDIX I.

incorruptible, invisible, the only God, *be* [*is*] honour and glory for ever and ever. Amen.'

1 Tim. vi. 15: 'He shall show, who is the blessed and only Potentate, the King of kings, and Lord of lords; who alone hath immortality, dwelling in light unapproachable; whom no man hath seen, nor can see: to whom *be* [*is*] honour and power eternal. Amen.'

2 Tim. iv. 18: 'To whom *be* [*is*] the glory for ever and ever. Amen.' [In this passage 'to whom' refers to ὁ Κύριος, and it is possible to contend that this means the Lord Jesus Christ. Careful examination of the epistle will not, I think, lead to this conclusion. Jesus is twice called 'our Lord' (i. 2, 8); but 'the Lord,' so frequently recurring, generally (*see* i. 18; ii. 7, 14, 19, 22) *must* mean God, and *may* do so always.]

All these doxologies, then, with their solemn Amens, are to the honour of God supreme, not of ὁ Κύριος Ἰησοῦς Χριστός.

Heb. xiii. 21 is ambiguous; and although I am convinced that ᾧ (*to whom*) refers to the subject ὁ Θεός, some may choose to contend that it belongs to the proximate Ἰησοῦ Χριστοῦ.

Compare 1 Pet. v. 11: 'To Him [God] *be* [*is*] the dominion for ever and ever. Amen.'

Jude 25: 'To the only God our Saviour, through Jesus Christ our Lord, *be* [*is*] glory, majesty, dominion, and power, before all time, and now and for evermore. Amen.'

In 2 Pet. iii. 18 the doxology is to 'our Lord and Saviour Jesus Christ.' But this epistle was one of the ancient ἀντιλεγόμενα, and among those who have denied its genuineness are Calvin, Neander, and Olshausen.

Those who, after examining all these passages (to which many might have been added), and weighing the intrinsic probability founded on their accumulated evidence, can approve the authorised text and translation in Rom. ix. 5, or the revised translation in Tit. ii. 13, have minds very differently constituted from mine. If St. Paul, in the outset of his epistle, doctrinally declares his Good-tidings concerning the Son of God, Jesus Christ our Lord; and after speaking of Him, κατὰ σάρκα, as in ix. 5, does not add that He is Θεὸς (κατὰ πνεῦμα), but υἱὸς Θεοῦ, how can those who have a satisfactory alternative be expected to believe that in ix. 5 he all of a sudden calls the Christ 'God over all, blessed for ever'?

And this he is supposed to do in a place where he is consoling the Jews by enumerating their many and great privileges, especially that of being the countrymen of ὁ Χριστὸς τὸ κατὰ σάρκα. If indeed the Jews of St. Paul's time had been expecting their Messiah to be the supreme God (ὁ ἐπὶ πάντων) manifest in the flesh, there might be some ground for maintaining the ascription. But no such expectation existed among them. Of an incarnate God they had no idea, no anticipation.

The interpretation which I support is in striking harmony with Eph. iv. 4–6: ἓν σῶμα καὶ ἓν Πνεῦμα, καθὼς καὶ ἐκλήθητε ἐν μιᾷ ἐλπίδι τῆς κλήσεως ὑμῶν·

εἷς Κύριος, μία πίστις, ἓν βάπτισμα, εἷς Θεὸς καὶ πατὴρ πάντων, ὁ ἐπὶ πάντων, καὶ διὰ πάντων, καὶ ἐν πᾶσιν. As, in recounting Jewish privileges, he crowns the list by saying that God (the one God of Israel) is 'over all,' so here, recounting Christian privileges, St. Paul adds that God the Father (of His redeemed children) is 'over all,' and more than this, is 'through all and in them all' (*i.e.* by His Holy Spirit).

Lachmann and Meyer are among the most eminent interpreters who punctuate fully after σάρκα. But the revised margin is not accurate in ascribing this view to moderns only. See the second volume of Professors Westcott and Hort: Introduction and Appendix to their Text of the N. T. At p. 109, stating the external evidence on this question, they show that the oldest Greek MSS., Aleph, B, A, have no punctuation in the passage, but that C (Codex Ephraemi) and some good cursives have a full stop after σάρκα. This is quite sufficient to prove the existence of the interpretation for which I contend before the fifth century. A probability is also shown that Origen held this opinion. And Dr. Hort himself says that such punctuation alone seems adequate to account for the whole of the language employed, more especially when it is considered in relation to the context.

Finally, this passage can never be cited in any controversy: for the other party would at once deny the 'orthodox' punctuation and translation to be correct; and by what force of argument is he to be silenced, when manuscripts prove nothing on one side or on the other, and internal probability is all in all? Is any *good* purpose served by clinging to untenable interpretations, any more than to untenable readings? 'Sursum corda!'[1]

[1] In Matt. i. 20 and Luke i. 35 the Authorised translators have rendered Hagion Pneuma '*the* Holy Ghost,' though it has no article: and the Revisers follow them. In Tit. ii. 13 they have not carried on τοῦ to Σωτῆρος: the Revisers have carried it on, and are applauded as giving 'a more clear declaration of the Godhead of Christ.' This 'clutching at straws' does not seem to serve the cause of orthodoxy, but to damage it. If St. Paul had called our Saviour θεός in these places, as He is more than once called in St. John's Gospel, this would not prove that the apostles and their age had been taught to look behind the veil of that great μυστήριον θεότητος. It would still be true that the logical definitions of our creeds, drawn from Scriptural data, grew in later days out of the need felt in the Church of silencing the over-curious speculations of erring men. But let it be seen that all those data are sound. Bishop Shuttleworth was a learned and candid divine; but in his Paraphrase of the Epistles, p. 345, he writes, on 1 Tim. iii. 16, 'If we admit the commonly received and more probable reading, Θεός, in preference to the ὅς contended for *by the Socinians*, it will form an epitome of belief consisting of the following articles: first, the divinity and incarnation of Christ,' &c., &c. And ὅς is now allowed by all wise and candid divines of our Church to be the true reading. Since the μυστήριον is Christ himself, there is not the very slightest difficulty in its being referred to by a masculine relative.

APPENDIX II.

THE following paper by Professor Ezra Abbot, D.D., LL.D., is reprinted from the *Sunday School Times* of May 21, 1881, p. 340:—

A VERY important part of the work of the new revision has consisted in the settlement of the Greek text to be followed in the translation. This was a duty which could not be evaded. To undertake to correct merely the mistranslations in the common English version, without reference to the question of the genuineness of the text, would be equivalent to saying that, while the mistakes of translators must be rectified, those of transcribers and editors should be regarded as sacred. It would be deliberately imposing on the Christian public hundreds of readings which all intelligent scholars, on the ground of decisive evidence, now agree in rejecting as spurious.

That there should be many mistakes in our manuscripts of the Greek New Testament, as there are in all other manuscripts of ancient authors, and that a portion of these mistakes should be capable of correction only by the comparison of many different copies, was inevitable in the nature of things, unless a perpetual miracle should be wrought. That such a miracle has not been wrought is shown by the multitude of 'various readings' which a comparison of copies has actually brought to light, the number of which was roughly reckoned at thirty thousand in the days of Mill (1707), and may now be estimated at not fewer than one hundred thousand.

This host of various readings may startle one who is not acquainted with the subject, and he may imagine that the whole text of the New Testament is thus rendered uncertain. But a careful analysis will show that nineteen-twentieths of these are of no more consequence than the palpable errata in the first proof of a modern printer; they have so little authority, or are so manifestly false, that they may be at once dismissed from consideration. Of those which remain, probably nine-tenths are of no importance as regards the sense; the differences either cannot be represented in a translation, or affect the form of expression merely, not the essential meaning of the sentence. Though the corrections made by the revisers in the Greek text of the New Testament followed by our translators exceed five thousand hardly one-tenth of them will be noticed by the ordinary reader. Of the residue, many are indeed of sufficient interest and importance to constitute one of the strongest reasons for making a new revision, which should no longer suffer the known errors of copyists to take the place of the words of the evangelists and apostles. But the chief value of the work accomplished by the self-denying scholars who have spent so much time and labour in the search for manuscripts, and in their collation or publication, does not

consist, after all, in the corrections of the text which
have resulted from their researches. These corrections may affect a few of the passages which have
been relied on for the support of certain doctrines,
but not to such an extent as essentially to alter the
state of the question. Still less is any question of
Christian duty touched by the multitude of various
readings. The greatest service which the scholars
who have devoted themselves to critical studies and
the collection of critical materials have rendered, has
been the establishment of the fact that, on the whole,
the New Testament writings have come down to us
in a text remarkably free from important corruptions,
even in the late and inferior manuscripts on which
the so-called 'received text' was founded; while the
helps which we now possess for restoring it to its
primitive purity far exceed those which we enjoy in
the case of any important classical author whose
works have come down to us. The multitude of
'various readings,' which to the thoughtless or
ignorant seems so alarming, is simply the result of
the extraordinary richness and variety of our critical
resources.

At this point it may be well to illustrate, by a
brief statement, the difference between the position of
the present revisers and King James's translators 270
years ago, as regards a critical knowledge of the
Greek text of the New Testament. The translators
or revisers of 1611 followed strictly no one edition of
the Greek Testament, though their revision seems to
agree more closely, on the whole, with Beza's later
editions (1588 and 1598) than with any other. But

APPENDIX II.

Beza's various editions (1565-98, fol. 1565-1604, 8vo) were founded mainly on Robert Stephens's editions of 1550 and 1551. For those editions Stephens had a very imperfect collation of fifteen manuscripts from the Royal Library at Paris, and of the Complutensian Polyglot, whose readings were given in his margin. Of his manuscripts, ten contained the Gospels, eight the Acts and Epistles, and two the Apocalypse. Two of these manuscripts of the Gospels were valuable (D and L), but he made very little use of them; indeed, the manuscript readings given in his margin seem in general to have served rather for show than for use. Scrivener has noted 119 places in which his text is in opposition to all of them. That text is, in fact, substantially formed from the last editions of Erasmus (1527-35), which differ very slightly from each other. Now what was Erasmus's critical apparatus? In the Gospels he had, all told, three manuscripts,—one of the tenth century, and a good one, but which he hardly ever followed, because its text seemed so peculiar that he was afraid of it. He used as the basis of his text in the Gospels an inferior manuscript of the fifteenth century. In the Acts and Catholic Epistles he had four modern manuscripts; in the Pauline Epistles, five; in the Revelation, only one, an inaccurate copy of which was used by the printer. This manuscript was mutilated, lacking the last six verses of the book, which Erasmus supplied by *translating* back from the Latin Vulgate into pretty bad Greek. This was not all. In other passages he took the liberty of correcting or supplementing his text from the Latin Vulgate;

APPENDIX II.   95

Beza occasionally took a similar liberty; and the result is, that in a considerable number of cases, not, indeed, in general of much importance, the reading of the common English version is *supported by no known Greek manuscript*, but rests on an error of Erasmus or Beza (for example, Acts ix. 5, 6; Rom. vii. 6; 2 Cor. i. 6; 1 Pet. iii. 20; Rev. i. 9, 11; ii. 3, 20, 24; iii. 2; v. 10, 14; xv. 3; xvi. 5; xvii. 8, 16; xviii. 2, &c.). Such is the foundation of the text on which the so-called Authorised Version was based.

It is impossible, without entering into tedious detail, to give an adequate idea of the immense accession to our critical resources which has resulted from the lifelong labours of generations of scholars since our common version was made. I will merely allude to Mill's edition of the Greek Testament (1707), on which he spent thirty years, mainly in collecting materials; to Bengel (1734), who did much to establish correct principles of criticism; to Wetstein, whose magnificent edition of the Greek Testament (1751-52), in two folio volumes, represents the arduous labour of forty years, and who added greatly to our knowledge of manuscripts, and the quotations of the Christian fathers; and to the extensive collations of manuscripts by Alter, Birch, with his associates, and Matthæi, the latter of whom alone carefully examined more than one hundred. Above all his predecessors, Griesbach stands pre-eminent. He not only added much to the materials already collected, but was the first to turn them to proper account in the correction of the received text, and in critical tact has perhaps been excelled by none of those who have succeeded him. After Griesbach, who links the last to the present century, we may name the Roman Catholic Scholz, a poor critic, but who brought to light and partially collated many hundreds of manuscripts before undescribed; Lachmann, the eminent classical scholar, whose original genius gave a new impulse to textual criticism; Scrivener, to whom we are indebted for excellent editions of two important uncial manuscripts (the Codex Bezæ or Cambridge manuscript of the Gospels and the Acts, and the Codex Augiensis of the Pauline Epistles), and for the careful collation of about seventy cursive manuscripts; and, above all, Tischendorf and Tregelles, whose indefatigable labours have made an epoch in the history of New Testament criticism. To describe these labours here in detail is utterly out of the question. It may suffice to say that, for the purpose of enlarging and perfecting our critical apparatus, Tischendorf visited nearly all the principal libraries of Europe, collating or copying for publication the most important manuscripts of the New Testament, whose text had not before been printed. Besides this, he took three journeys to the East, bringing home rich manuscript treasures, and crowning all with the magnificent discovery of the Sinai manuscript, of the fourth century, containing the New Testament absolutely complete. He spent more than eight years in these travels and collations. His editions of the texts of Biblical manuscripts, published by him for the first time, or for the first time accurately, comprise no less than seventeen large quarto and five folio volumes, not counting the 'Anecdota Sacra et Profana,' and the 'Notitia editionis Codicis Sinaitici,' two quarto volumes containing descriptions or collations of many new manuscripts. Many of his collations, or copies of important manuscripts, still remain unpublished, though used in his last critical edition of the Greek Testament. Between the years 1840 and 1873 he issued as many as twenty-four editions of the Greek New Testament, including the re-impressions of his stereotyped *editio academica*. Only four of these editions, however, those of 1841, 1849, 1859, and 1869-72, are independently important, as marking great advances in the acquisition of new materials. The mere catalogue of Tischendorf's publications, prepared by Dr. Gregory for the *Bibliotheca Sacra* (January 1876), most of them relating to Biblical criticism, covers more than ten octavo pages.

Dr. Tregelles, like Tischendorf, visited many of the principal European libraries, making three journeys to the Continent for this purpose, and collated with extreme care the most important uncial manuscripts, and a number of very valuable cursives. He compared his collations with those of Tischendorf, and, in case of any discrepancy, settled the question by a re-examination of the manuscript. The only new manuscript which he published was the Codex Zacynthius, a palimpsest of great value belonging to the library of the British and Foreign Bible Society, and containing about a third of the Gospel of Luke. He issued but one edition of the Greek Testament (1857-72), and was disabled by paralysis from person-

H

ally completing the Prolegomena or Introduction to this, and from supplying the needful corrections and additions. His accuracy in the statement of his authorities, and the new material incorporated in the notes, give the work great value, and the arrangement of the matter is very lucid. But though not to be compared with Tischendorf in the extent of his contributions to our stock of critical material, Dr. Tregelles did far more than his rival to illustrate and enforce the principles on which a critical edition of the Greek Testament should be based, and to establish, by what he called 'comparative criticism,' the right of a few of the oldest manuscripts, in many cases, to outweigh a vast numerical majority of later authorities. He did far more, probably, than any other writer, to overcome the blind and unreasoning prejudice which so long existed in England in favour of the so-called 'received text.'

A rough account of the number of Greek manuscripts of the New Testament now known will give some idea of the vast enlargement of our critical materials since the time when the common English version was made. We have now for the Gospels 60 uncials (reckoning the six Psalters, &c., which contain the hymns in Luke i. 46-55, 68-79; ii. 29-32), ranging from the fourth century to the tenth, and more than 600 cursives, dating from the tenth century to the sixteenth; for the Acts and Catholic Epistles, seventeen uncials and over 200 cursives; for the Pauline Epistles, twenty uncials and over 280 cursives; for the Revelation, five uncials and about 100 cursives. To these are to be added over 340

APPENDIX II. 99

Evangelistaries and about eighty Praxapostoli; that is, manuscripts containing the Lessons from the Gospels and the Acts and Epistles read in the service of the church. This very rough statement, however, requires much qualification to prevent a false impression, as more than half of the uncials are mere fragments, though very valuable fragments, and most of the others are more or less mutilated; while a large majority of the cursives have been but partially collated, or only inspected. But *all* of the uncials, incomparably the most valuable part of the apparatus, have been thoroughly collated (with the exception of the recently discovered Codex Rossanensis); indeed, the whole text of the most valuable among them has been published.

There is another very important class of our critical documents which can be noticed only in the briefest manner. The translations of the New Testament into different languages, made at an early date for the benefit of Christian converts ignorant of Greek —the *ancient versions*, as they are commonly termed— represent the text current in widely separated regions of the Christian world, and are often of the highest importance in settling questions of textual criticism. Two of these versions, the Old Latin and the Curetonian Syriac, belong to the second century; two, the Memphitic or Coptic, and the Thebaic or Sahidic, to the earlier part of the third; four more, the Peshito Syriac in its present form, the Gothic, the Latin Vulgate, and the Ethiopic (perhaps) to the fourth; two, the Armenian and the Jerusalem Syriac, to the fifth; and there are several other later versions of considerable importance, as the Philoxenian or Harclean Syriac and the Slavonic. The earlier editors of the Greek Testament knew none of these except the Vulgate and the Peshito, and the former only in a very corrupt text. They made little use of either of them, except occasionally to corrupt the Greek text from the more familiar Vulgate. The Curetonian Syriac is a recent discovery; and the value of this and of the other early versions in textual criticism can hardly be overestimated. Our knowledge of the Old Latin version or versions has been very greatly extended by the labours of scholars in the present century in connection with the discovery of new manuscripts.

A third and also very important class of our authorities consists of the numerous *quotations* of the New Testament by early Christian writers, many of them one or two centuries earlier than the date of our oldest manuscripts. In respect to these, though Mill, Bengel, Wetstein, Sabatier, Griesbach, Matthæi, and others had made extensive collections, our critical apparatus has been greatly augmented by the labours of Tischendorf and Tregelles.

The most valuable result of these vast accessions to our critical apparatus has been indirect rather than direct. It has enabled us to trace the outlines of the history of the text; to determine, approximately, the *relative value* of our different authorities and their distinguishing characteristics; it has enabled us to establish on a solid foundation certain *principles of criticism*, which serve as a guide through the labyrinth of conflicting testimonies.

APPENDIX III.

SELECT TEXTUAL CORRECTIONS

in the REVISED VERSION *of the* NEW TESTAMENT.

[The Former Column gives the English of the Authorised Version: the Revised Correction stands in the opposite Column. A (Absent) implies that the Authorised word or words were omitted in the Revision by preponderant authorities.]

MATTHEW.

CHAPTER I.

25   her firstborn son: . . . | a son:

CHAPTER II.

18   lamentation and . . . | A

CHAPTER III.

6   in Jordan, . . . | in the river Jordan,

CHAPTER V.

21   by them . . . . | to them
22   without a cause . . . | A
27   by them of old time, . . | A
30   be cast . . . . . | go
44   bless them that curse you, do good to them that hate you, | A
—   which . . . . . | that
—   despitefully use you and . . | A
47   publicans so? . . . . | Gentiles the same?

Chapter VI.

1	alms	righteousness
4	himself	A
4, 6, 18	shall reward thee openly.	shall recompense thee.
5	when thou prayest, thou shalt	when ye pray, ye shall
12	as we forgive	as we also have forgiven
13	for thine is . . . . Amen. .	A
21	your . . . . your . .	thy . . . . thy
25	and	or
33	the kingdom of God, . .	his kingdom,
34	for the things of itself. . .	for itself.

Chapter VII.

2	to you again.	unto you.
24	I will liken him . . .	shall be likened
24, 25	a rock	the rock
29	the scribes.	their scribes.

Chapter VIII.

15	unto them.	unto him.
28	Gergesenes, ...	Gadarenes,
31	suffer us to go. . . .	send us
32	into the herd of swine. . .	into the swine.
—	the whole herd of swine . .	the whole herd

Chapter IX.

8	they marvelled, . . .	they were afraid,
13	to repentance. . . .	A
35	among the people. . .	A
36	fainted and were scattered abroad, ...	were distressed and scattered,

Chapter X.

3	Lebbæus, whose surname was	A
4	Canaanite, ...	Cananæan,
10	staves :	staff :
23	another :	the next :

SELECT TEXTUAL CORRECTIONS. 103

CHAPTER XI.

2	two of	by
9	but what went ye out for to see? A prophet?	but wherefore went ye out? to see a prophet?
—	more	much more
16	and calling	which call
19	of her children. . . .	by her works.
23	which art exalted unto heaven, shalt be brought down to hell:	shalt thou be exalted to heaven? thou shalt go down unto Hades.

CHAPTER XIII.

9, 43	to hear	A
44	Again	A
46	who	and
51	Jesus saith unto them, . .	A
—	Lord.	A

CHAPTER XIV.

6	was kept, ...	came,
13	by ship, ...	in a boat,
30	boisterous	A
32	come	gone up
33	came and	A
34	into the land of . . .	to the land, unto

CHAPTER XV.

4	commanded, saying . .	said
6	and honour not his father or his mother, he shall be free.	he shall not honour his father.
—	the commandment . . .	the word
8	draweth nigh unto me with their mouth, and . . .	A
14	of the blind	A
17	yet	A
39	Magdala.	Magadan.

CHAPTER XVI.

3	O ye hypocrites, . . .	A
4	the prophet	A
13	whom do men say that I the Son of man am?	who do men say that the Son of man is?
26	lose his own soul? . . .	forfeit his life?

Chapter XVII.

4	let us make	I will make
10	first.	A
20	unbelief:	little faith:
21	Howbeit .... fasting.	A
26	Peter saith unto him, Of strangers.	And when he said, From strangers,

Chapter XVIII.

11	For .... lost.	A
29	at his feet	A
—	all.	A
35	their trespasses.	A

Chapter XIX.

16	Good Master,	Master,
17	Why callest thou me good? there is none good but one, that is, God:	Why askest thou me concerning that which is good? One there is who is good:
20	from my youth up	A
29	or wife	A

Chapter XX.

6	standing idle,	standing;
7	and .... receive	A
16	for many .... chosen.	A
17	in the way, and	, and in the way he
22	and to be .... with?	A
23	and be .... with:	A
26, 27	let him be	shall be
30, 31	have mercy on us, O Lord,	Lord, have mercy on us,
34	their eyes	they

Chapter XXI.

7	they set him	he sat
13	have made	make
15	crying	that were crying

Chapter XXII.

7	when the king heard thereof, he	the king
13	take him away, and	A
30	the angels of God	angels

SELECT TEXTUAL CORRECTIONS.   105

35	and saying, ...	A
39	the second is like unto it, .	a second like *unto it* is this,
40	hang	hangeth
44	make	put
—	thy footstool.	underneath thy feet.

CHAPTER XXIII.

3	observe, that observe and do ;	, these do and observe :
7	Rabbi, Rabbi.. . . .	Rabbi.
8	Master, ...	teacher,
—	even Christ ;	A
14	Woe . . . . damnation. . .	A
17	sanctifieth	hath sanctified
19	fools and	A

CHAPTER XXIV.

2	And Jesus said . . .	But he answered and said
17	to take anything out of his house :	to take out the things that are in his house :
18	clothes.	cloke.
36	but my Father . . .	neither the Son, but the Father
42	what hour	on what day

CHAPTER XXV.

6	cometh ;	A
13	wherein . . . . cometh. . .	A
15	and straightway took his journey.	and he went on his journey.
16	Then he that had . . .	Straightway he that
20, 22	beside them	A
31	holy	A

CHAPTER XXVI.

3	and the scribes, . . .	A
20	he sat down with the twelve. .	he was sitting at meat with the twelve disciples.
28	of the new testament, . .	of the covenant,
42	cup . . . . from me, . .	cannot pass away,
43	he came	he came again
—	asleep again ;	sleeping,
44	he left them, ...	he left them again,

44	went away again, . .	went away,
50	wherefore art thou come? .	*do* that for which thou art come.
53	now pray to	beseech
—	presently give	even now send
55	with you	A
59	and elders, ...	A
60	came two false witnesses, .	came two,
63	answered and	A

Chapter XXVII.

5	in the temple, . . .	into the sanctuary,
23	the governor said, . . .	he said,
35	that it might be . . . . lots. .	A
42	If he be	He is
58	the body to be delivered. .	it to be given up.
64	by night	A

Chapter XXVIII.

2	from the door, . . .	A
9	as they went to tell his disciples, ...	A
17	him, ...	A
20	Amen.	A

MARK.

Chapter I.

2	in the prophets, . . .	in Isaiah the prophet,
4	John did baptize . . .	John came, who baptized
5	they of	all they of
—	and were all	and they were
11	in whom	in thee
13	there	A
14	of the kingdom . . .	A
16	his brother	the brother of Simon
19	thence, ...	A
23	there was	straightway there was
24	Let us alone ;	A
27	what thing is this? what new doctrine is this? . .	what is this? a new doctrine?
31	immediately	A

SELECT TEXTUAL CORRECTIONS.

39	he preached in their synagogues .... and cast out	he went into their synagogues ... preaching and casting out
42	as soon as he had spoken,	A

CHAPTER II.

2	straightway	A
7	blasphemies?	he blasphemeth;
16	the scribes and Pharisees	the scribes of the Pharisees
17	to repentance	A
18	And the disciples of John and of the Pharisees	And John's disciples and the Pharisees
22	new	A
—	doth burst	will burst
—	the wine is spilled, and the bottles will be marred :	the wine perisheth, and the skins :

CHAPTER III.

5	whole as the other.	A
15	to heal sicknesses, and	A
18	Canaanite,	Canaæan,
29	is in danger of eternal damnation :	is guilty of an eternal sin :

CHAPTER IV.

1	was gathered	is gathered
10	parable.	parables.
12	their sins	it
15	that was sown in their hearts.	which hath been sown in them.
19	this world,	the world,
20	some thirtyfold, some sixty, and some an hundred.	thirtyfold and sixtyfold and a hundredfold.
22	which shall not be	save that it should be
30	with what comparison shall we compare it?	in what parable shall we set it forth?
31	is less	though it be less
32	but when it is sown, it groweth up	yet, when it is sown, groweth up
34	his	his own
36	there were also with him other little ships.	other boats were with him.
37	it was now full.	the boat was now filling.

Chapter V.

1	Gadarenes.	Gerasenes.
3	could bind him, no, not with chains:	could any more bind him, no, not with a chain:
11	nigh unto the mountains	on the mountain side
13	And forthwith Jesus	And he
—	they were about	in number about
14	the swine	them
15	and clothed	clothed
22	And, behold,	And
23	and she shall live	and live
27	of Jesus,	the things concerning Jesus,
33	in her	to her
36	As soon as Jesus heard the word that was spoken,	But Jesus, not heeding (?) the word spoken,
38	he cometh	they come
40	lying.	A
42	astonished	amazed straightway

Chapter VI.

2	unto him, that even such mighty works are	unto this man? and what mean such mighty works
9	and not put on	and, *said he*, put not on
11	whosoever	whatsoever place
—	Verily . . . . that city.	A
15	or as	even as
16	It is John . . . . he is risen from the dead.	John . . . . he is risen.
20	he did many things	he was much perplexed
22	and pleased	she pleased
—	the king	and the king
26	sat with him,	sat at meat,
27	his head to be brought:	to bring his head:
36	bread: for they have nothing to eat.	somewhat to eat.
39	to make all	that all should
43	twelve baskets full of the fragments,	broken pieces, twelve basketfuls,
48	he saw . . . . and about .	seeing . . . . about

SELECT TEXTUAL CORRECTIONS.

51	beyond measure, and wondered.	A
52	for their heart . . .	but their heart
53	into the land of Gennesaret, .	to the land unto Gennesaret,

CHAPTER VII.

1, 2	which came from Jerusalem. And when they saw some	which had come from Jerusalem, and had seen that some
—	eat	ate
—	they found fault. . . .	A
4	and of tables. . . .	A
8	as the washing . . . . ye do. .	A
12	And (*the erasure of this particle changes the construction of* 11-12, *and renders the added* 'he shall be free' *needless* .	A
16	If any man . . . . hear. . .	A
19	purging all meats ? . . .	this he said, making all meats clean.
25	For a certain woman . .	But straightway a woman
—	heard of him, and came . .	having heard of him, came
30	the devil gone out, and her daughter laid upon the bed.	the child laid upon the bed, and the devil gone out.
31	of Tyre and Sidon, he came .	of Tyre, he came through Sidon
35	straightway	A

CHAPTER VIII.

1	the multitude being very great,	when there was again a great multitude,
9	that had eaten . . .	A
17	yet	A
21	how is it that ye do not understand ?	do ye not yet understand ?
22	he cometh	they come
24	I see men as trees, . . .	I see men, for I behold them as trees,
25	made him look up : . .	he looked stedfastly,
—	every man	all things
26	neither go into the town, .	do not even enter into the village.
—	nor tell it . . . . in the town. .	A
36	shall it . . . . . , .	doth it

36	if he shall	to
—	lose his own soul ? . . .	forfeit his life ?
37	or what shall	for what should
—	soul ?	life ?

Chapter IX.

3	as snow ;	A
6	to say ;	to answer ;
—	were	became
7	there was	there came
9	came	were coming
16	the scribes, ...	them,
23	if thou canst believe, . .	if thou canst !
24	with tears, Lord, . . .	A
26	was	became
28	why could not we cast him out?	we could not cast it out.
29	and fasting.	A
31	(x. 34) the third day . .	after three days
33	he came	they came
—	among yourselves . . .	A
38	and he followeth not us ; .	A
—	because he followeth not .	because he followed not
44, 46	Where . . . . quenched. .	A
49	and every sacrifice . . . . salt.	A

Chapter X.

1	by the farther side of . .	and beyond
6	God made them male and female.	male and female made he them.
8	be	become
10	the same.	this
12	a woman	she herself
21	take up the cross, and . .	A
29	or wife	A
46	blind Bartimæus, the son of Timæus,	the son of Timæus, Bartimæus, a blind beggar,
—	begging.	A
49	commanded him to be called.	said, Call ye him.
50	rose	sprang up

Chapter XI.

6	commanded :	said :
8	others cut down branches off the trees,	others branches which they had cut from the fields.
—	and strawed them in the way .	A
10	in the name of the Lord : .	A
11	and into the temple : . .	into the temple:
23	those things which . . .	what
—	whatsoever he saith. . .	it.
24	ye desire, when ye pray, .	ye pray and ask for,
26	But if . . . . your trespasses. .	A
29	also	A

Chapter XII.

4	and at him they cast stones, and wounded him in the head, and sent him away shamefully handled.	and him they wounded in the head, and handled shamefully.
6	Having yet therefore one son, his wellbeloved, . . .	He had yet one, a beloved son :
—	also	A
17	marvelled	marvelled greatly
19	children, ...	child,
21	neither left he any seed: .	leaving no seed behind him:
22	had her, and	A
23	therefore, when they shall rise	A
25	the angels which are . .	angels
27	but the God of the living : .	but of the living :
—	therefore	A
30	this is the first commandment.	A
31	and the second is like, namely this, ...	the second is this :
32	Well, Master, thou hast said the truth : for there is one God ;	Of a truth, Master, thou hast well said that he is one ;
33	and with all the soul, . .	A
—	more	much more

Chapter XIII.

8	and troubles :	A
14	spoken of by Daniel the prophet, ...	A

18	your flight	it
22	even	A
25	the stars of heaven shall fall,	the stars shall be falling from heaven,
27	his angels,	the angels,
32	and.	or
34	the Son of man is as	it is as when

Chapter XIV.

19	and another said, Is it I?	A
22	eat.	A
24	of the new testament,	of the covenant,
27	because of me this night:	A
31	the more	A
40	And when he returned,	And he came again,
—	asleep again,	sleeping,
43	great	A
45	Master, Master;	Rabbi;
51	the young men	they
52	from them	A
65	the servants did strike him with the palms of their hands.	the officers received him with blows of their hands.
70	and thy speech agreeth thereto.	A
72	And the second time	And straightway the second time

Chapter XV.

3	but he answered nothing.	A
7	with him,	A
8	crying aloud	went up and
—	as he had ever done	as he was wont to do
24	when they had crucified him, they parted.	they crucify him, and part
28	And the.... transgressors.	A

LUKE.

Chapter I.

1	are most surely believed.	have been fulfilled
28	blessed art thou among women.	A
29	when she saw him,	A
35	of thee	A

SELECT TEXTUAL CORRECTIONS.   113

37	with God nothing shall be impossible.	no word from God shall be void of power.
42	voice, ...	cry,
50	from generation to generation.	unto generations and generations.
75	all the days of our life. . .	all our days.
78	hath visited	shall visit

CHAPTER II.

5	Mary his espoused wife . .	Mary, who was betrothed to him,
9	behold	A
12	lying	and lying
14	good will towards men. . .	peace among men in whom he is well pleased.
21	of the child, ...	him,
22	her	their
33	Joseph	his father
37	she was a widow of about .	she had been a widow for
40	in spirit	A
42	to Jerusalem	A
43	Joseph and his mother . .	his parents

CHAPTER III.

2	Annas and Caiaphas being the high priests,	in the high-priesthood of Annas and Caiaphas,

CHAPTER IV.

1	into the wilderness. . .	in the wilderness.
4	but by every word of God .	A
5	And the devil, taking him up into an high mountain .	And he led him up and
8	Get thee behind me, Satan: for	A
18	to heal the brokenhearted .	A
26	to Sarepta, a city of Sidon, .	to Zarephath in the land of Sidon,
41	Thou art Christ the Son of God.	Thou art the Son of God.
43	am I sent.	was I sent.

CHAPTER V.

33	Why do	A
36	if otherwise, then . . . . a rent,	else he will rend the new,
38	and both are preserved. . .	A
39	straightway	A
—	better.	good.

I

Chapter VI.

1	the second .... first, . .	a Sabbath,
10	whole as the other . . .	A
16	also	A
26	so	in the same manner
35	hoping for nothing again; .	never despairing (?) ;
45	evil treasure of his heart . .	evil *treasure*
48	for it was founded upon a rock.	because it had been well builded.

Chapter VII.

10	that was sick	A
11	the day after, ...	soon afterwards,
—	many of	A
19	to Jesus, ...	to the Lord,
28	there is not .... the Baptist:	there is none greater than John:
31	And the Lord said . . .	A
42	Tell me therefore, which of them	Which of them therefore
44	with the hairs of her head. .	with her hair.

Chapter VIII.

3	unto him	unto them
20	by certain which said . .	A
26, 37	Gadarenes	Gerasenes
27	long time, and . . .	and for a long time
34	and went	A
40	it came to pass, that, when Jesus was returned, . . .	as Jesus returned,
45	and sayest thou, Who touched me?	A
48	be of good comfort . . .	A
54	put them all out, and . .	A

Chapter IX.

1	his twelve disciples, . .	the twelve,
3	staves, ...	staff,
7	by him	A
10	went aside privately into a desert place belonging to the city called Bethsaida.	withdrew apart to a city called Bethsaida.
35	my beloved Son: . . .	my Son, my chosen:

SELECT TEXTUAL CORRECTIONS.

38	look	to look
48	shall be great. . . .	is great.
50	not against us is for us. . .	not against you is for you.
54	even as Elias did . . .	A
55, 56	and said . . . . to save them	A
57	it came to pass . . .	A
—	Lord	A

CHAPTER X.

1	also	A
11	on us	to our feet
—	unto you	A
15	which art	shalt thou be
—	thrust down to hell. . .	brought down to Hades.
20	rather	A
21	in the spirit, ...	in the Holy Spirit,
32	when he was at the place, came	when he came to the place,
35	when he departed . . .	A
38	it came to pass . . .	A

CHAPTER XI.

2	Our Father which art in heaven,	Father,
—	Thy will . . . . heaven. . .	A
4	lead	bring
—	but deliver us from evil . .	A
29	the prophet	A
33	secret place, ...	cellar,
44	scribes . . . . hypocrites .	A
53	as he said these things unto them,	when he was come out from thence,
54	that they might accuse him. .	A

CHAPTER XII.

18	fruits	corn
31	all	A
56	do not discern . . .	know not how to interpret

CHAPTER XIII.

| 9 | well: and if not, then after that thou shalt cut it down. . | thenceforth, *well*; but if not, thou shalt cut it down. |
| 15 | thou hypocrite, . . . | ye hypocrites, |

19	great	A
25	Lord, Lord	Lord
31	The same day . . .	In that very hour
35	verily	A
—	the time come when . .	A

Chapter XIV.

3	on the sabbath day? . .	on the sabbath, or not?
10	of them	of all

Chapter XV.

16	filled his belly	been filled
21	make me as one of thy hired servants.	A
22	Bring forth	Bring forth quickly

Chapter XVI.

9	when ye fail, ...	when it shall fail,

Chapter XVII.

9	I trow not.	A
18	There are not found . .	Were there none found
21	lo there!	there!
23	See here; or, see there:	lo there, or lo here!
36	two men shall be . . . . left.	A

Chapter XVIII.

7	though he bear long with them?	and he is longsuffering over them?

Chapter XIX.

42	If thou hadst known, even thou, at least in this thy day, the things which belong unto thy peace!	if thou hadst known in this day, even thou, the things which belong unto peace!
45	therein, and them that bought	A
46	my house is	my house shall be

SELECT TEXTUAL CORRECTIONS.

CHAPTER XX.

13	when they see him.	A
14	come	A
23	Why tempt ye me?	A
30	and the second .... childless	and the second:
31	the seven also: and they left.	the seven also left
32	last of all	afterward
33	is she?	shall she be?

CHAPTER XXI.

4	unto the offerings of God	unto the gifts
11	in divers places, and famines.	and famines in divers places
25	with perplexity; the sea and the waves roaring;	in perplexity for the roaring of the sea and the billows;

CHAPTER XXII.

31	And the Lord said,.	A
61	crow,	crow this day,
62	Peter	he
64	they struck him on the face.	A
68	me, nor let me go;.	A

CHAPTER XXIII.

6	of Galilee,	it,
17	For of .... feast..	A
23	and of the chief priests.	A
38	in letters of Greek, and Latin, and Hebrew,	A
39	If thou be Christ,	Art not thou the Christ?
42	And he said unto Jesus, Lord,	And he said, Jesus,
—	into thy kingdom..	in thy kingdom.
45	And the sun was darkened,.	the sun's light failing:
54	that day was the preparation,.	it was the day of the Preparation,

CHAPTER XXIV.

1	and certain others with them.	A
10	, and other women that were with them, which told	: and the other women with them told
17	and are sad?.	And they stood still, looking sad.
42	and of an honeycomb..	A

APPENDIX III.

46	Thus it is written, and thus it behoved Christ to suffer,	Thus it is written, that the Christ should suffer,
49	of Jerusalem, ...	A
53	praising and	A
—	Amen.	A

JOHN.

CHAPTER I.

27	. He it is, who coming after me is preferred before me, .	, even he that cometh after me
29	John	he
42	of Jona :	of John :
43	and saith	and Jesus saith
49	and saith unto . . .	A
51	Hereafter	A

CHAPTER III.

15	in him should not perish, but .	may in him
25	the Jews	a Jew
32	And what	What

CHAPTER IV.

15	hither	all the way hither
17	said	said unto him
42	the Christ, ...	A
43	and went	A
51	and told him	A
—	Thy son liveth. . . .	that his son lived.

CHAPTER V.

3	great	A
4, 5	waiting for . . . . disease he had.	A
5	an infirmity thirty and eight years.	been thirty and eight years in his infirmity.
16	and sought to slay him, . .	A
27	also, ...	A
30	of the Father	of him

Chapter VI.

11	to the disciples, and the disciples	A
17	was not come	had not yet come
22	when	A
—	save that one	save one,
—	whereinto his disciples were entered	A
51	which I will give . . .	A
58	as your fathers did eat manna,	as the fathers did eat,
65	my Father	the Father.
69	that Christ, the Son of the living God	the Holy One of God.
71	Iscariot the son of Simon, .	the son of Simon Iscariot,

Chapter VII.

10	gone up, then went he also up unto the feast,	gone up unto the feast, then went he also up,
20	and said, ...	A
26	the very Christ ? . . .	the Christ ?
39	the Holy Ghost . . .	the Spirit
40	this saying, ...	these words,
46	spake like this man . . .	so spake.
50	by night	A
53	(to viii. 11)	(omitted by most ancient authorities, and varied by others: in R. V. printed within brackets)

Chapter VIII.

6	as though he heard them not .	A
9	being convicted by their own conscience, ...	A
—	standing	, where she was,
10	and saw none but the woman,	A
—	those thine accusers ? . .	they ?
11	sin no more.	from henceforth sin no more.
29	the Father hath not . .	he hath not
38	which ye have seen with your father.	which ye heard from your father.
44	abode not	stood not
59	going through the midst of them, and so passed by. .	A

Chapter IX.

6	the eyes of the blind man	his eyes
8	blind,	a beggar,
9	He is like him.	No, but he is like him.
11	the pool of	A

Chapter X.

12	scattereth the sheep:	scattereth them:
13	the hireling	he
26	as I said unto you.	A
38	and believe	and understand

Chapter XI.

22	But I know	And even now I know
31	saying, She goeth	supposing that she was going
41	from the place where the dead was laid.	A

Chapter XII.

1	which had been dead,	A
4	Simon's son,	A
7	Let her alone:	Suffer her to keep it:
—	hath she kept this	(Omit)
47	and believe not,	and keep them not,

Chapter XIII.

24	that he should ask who it should be of whom he spake.	and saith unto him, Tell us who it is of whom he speaketh.
25	He then lying.	He leaning back, as he was,
32	if God be glorified in him,	A

Chapter XIV.

5	ye know, and the way ye know.	the way ye know.
28	because I said, I go	because I go

Chapter XV.

11	that my joy might remain	that my joy may be

SELECT TEXTUAL CORRECTIONS.

CHAPTER XVI.

10	My Father, ...	the Father,
16	because I go to the Father. .	A
23	in my name, He will give it you.	, He will give it you in my name.
33	ye shall have	ye have

CHAPTER XVII.

4	I have	having
12	in the world	A
17	through thy truth: . . .	in the truth:
21	one in us:	in us:
24	I will that they also, whom thou hast given me, be with me where I am ;	that which thou hast given me, I will that, where I am, they also may be with me ;

CHAPTER XVIII.

20	the Jews always . . .	all the Jews
40	all	A

CHAPTER XIX.

3	and said, . . .	and they came unto him and said,
7	by our law	by that law

CHAPTER XX.

16	saith unto him, . .	saith unto him in Hebrew,
29	Thomas	A

CHAPTER XXI.

25	Amen.	A

ACTS.

CHAPTER I.

14	and supplication . . .	A
15	of the disciples, . . .	of the brethren,
19	proper	A
25	take part of	take the place in

Chapter II.

1	with one accord	together
7	one to another	A
30	according to the flesh, he would raise up Christ to sit on his throne;	he would set one upon his throne;
31	that his soul was not left in hell,	that neither was he left in Hades,
33	now.	A
41	gladly	A
47	And the Lord added to the church daily such as should be saved.	And the Lord added to them day by day those that were being saved.

Chapter III.

3	asked	asked to receive
6	rise up and walk.	walk.
11	the lame man which was healed	he
18	Christ	his Christ
20	he shall send Jesus Christ, which before was preached unto you:	that he may send the Christ who hath been appointed for you, even Jesus:
22	unto the fathers	A
—	the Lord your God	the Lord God
25	our fathers,	your fathers,
26	his Son Jesus	his Servant,

Chapter IV.

17	straitly	A
24	thou art God,	A
25	who by the mouth of thy servant David hast said,	who by the Holy Ghost, by the mouth of our father David thy servant, didst say,
27	of a truth	of a truth in this city
—	child	Servant

Chapter V.

5	these things.	it.
24	the high priest and	A
28	Did not we straitly command	We straitly charged
32	his witnesses	witnesses

SELECT TEXTUAL CORRECTIONS.

33	took counsel	were minded
34	the apostles	the men
37	much people	some of the people
39	overthrow it ;	overthrow them ;
42	Jesus Christ.	Jesus *as* the Christ.

CHAPTER VI.

3	of the Holy Ghost . . .	of the Spirit
8	of faith	of grace
13	blasphemous	A

CHAPTER VII.

17	had sworn to	vouchsafed unto
18	king	king over Egypt,
30	of the Lord	A
32	and the God of Isaac, and the God of Jacob. . . .	and of Isaac, and of Jacob.
35	did God send	hath God sent
37	the Lord your God . .	God
—	him shall ye hear. . . .	A
43	Remphan, ...	Rephan,

CHAPTER VIII.

7	(*text corrupt*) . . .	(*reading and version doubtful*)[1]
10	the great power of God. . .	that power of God which is called great.
13	beholding the miracles and signs which were done.	beholding signs and great miracles wrought.
22	God, ...	the Lord,
37	And Philip . . . . Son of God.	A

CHAPTER IX.

5	the Lord	he
5–6	it is hard . . . . said unto him,	A
6	Arise	But rise
8	no man :	nothing :
12	in a vision	A
—	hand	hands
18	forthwith, ...	A

[1] viii. 7. The readings now received afford no construction. Were the rel. ἁ supplied after ἀκάθαρτα, the verse might be construed.

19, 26	Saul	he
20	Christ	Jesus
21	came	he had come
25	the disciples	his disciples
31	the churches	the church
—	and were	being
—	were multiplied.	was multiplied.
38	desiring him that he would not delay to come unto them.	intreating him, Delay not to come unto us.

CHAPTER X.

6	he shall .... to do.	A
7	Cornelius	him
11	unto him,	A
—	knit at the four corners, and let down to .	let down by four corners upon
16	again	straightway
21	which were .... Cornelius ; .	A
23	Peter	he arose and
30	I was fasting until this hour; and at the ninth hour I prayed in my house,	until this hour, I was keeping the ninth hour of prayer in my house,
32	who, when he cometh, shall speak unto thee. .	A
33	of God.	of the Lord.
48	the Lord.	Jesus Christ.

CHAPTER XI.

11	where I was,	in which we were,
12	nothing doubting.	making no distinction.
21	believed, and	that believed
22	that he should go	A
25	Barnabas	he
28	Cæsar.	A

CHAPTER XIII.

19, 20	he divided their land to them by lot. And after that he gave unto them judges about the space of four hundred and fifty years,	he gave them their land for an inheritance, for about four hundred and fifty years : and after these things he gave them judges,

23	raised	brought
33	unto us their children, . .	unto our children,
35	Wherefore	Because
42	And when the Jews were gone out of the synagogue, the Gentiles besought	And as they went out, they besought

Chapter XIV.

28	there	A

Chapter XV.

11	Christ	A
17–18	who doeth all these things. Known unto God are all his works	who maketh these things known
23	letters after this manner ; .	thus
24	saying . . . . law : . .	A
33	unto the apostles. . . .	unto those that had sent them forth.
34	Notwithstanding . . . . still. .	A
37	determined	was minded
40	of God.	of the Lord.

Chapter XVI.

7	the Spirit	the Spirit of Jesus
10	the Lord	God
13	out of the city . . .	without the gate
—	where prayer was wont to be made ;	where we supposed there was a place of prayer ;
16	to prayer, ...	to the place of prayer,
17	unto us	unto you
31	Christ, ...	A

Chapter XVII.

5	which believed not, . .	A
13	and stirred up . . .	stirring up and troubling
26	blood	A

Chapter XVIII.

1	Paul	he
5	was pressed in the spirit,	was constrained by the word,
7	Justus, ...	Titus Justus,
21	bade them farewell, saying,	taking his leave of them, and saying,
—	I must by all means . . . . Jerusalem : but	A
22	and he sailed	, he set sail
25	the things of the Lord,	the things concerning Jesus,

Chapter XIX.

1-2	and finding certain disciples, he said unto them,	and found certain disciples: and he said unto them,
4	Christ Jesus.	Jesus.
9	one Tyrannus. . . .	Tyrannus.
10	Jesus, ...	A
13	We adjure	I adjure
16	overcame them, . . .	mastered both of them,
27	and her magnificence should be destroyed,	and that she should even be deposed from her magnificence,
35	goddess	A
40	there being no cause whereby we may give an account of this concourse.	there being no cause *for it*; and as touching it we shall not be able to give account of this concourse.

Chapter XX.

7	the disciples	we
8	they	we
15	and tarried at Trogyllium ;	A
24	But none of these things move me, neither count I my life dear unto myself,	But I hold not my life of any account as dear unto myself,
—	with joy, ...	A
25	of God, ...	A

Chapter XXI.

4	go up to	set foot in
5-6	and prayed. And . .	we prayed, and
8	that were of Paul's company .	A

SELECT TEXTUAL CORRECTIONS. 127

22	the multitude must needs come together:	A
25	and concluded that they observe no such thing, save only that they keep	giving judgment that they should keep

CHAPTER XXII.

16	the name of the Lord.	his name.
20	to his death,	A
30	from his bands,	A
—	to appear,	to come together,

CHAPTER XXIII.

9	but if .... to him,	and what if .... to him?
—	let us not fight against God.	A
20	they would	thou wouldest
30	that the Jews laid wait for the man,	that there would be a plot against the man,
—	farewell.	A
34	the governor .... the letter,	he .... it,

CHAPTER XXIV.

1	the elders	certain elders
2	very worthy deeds are done	evils are corrected
6-8	and would have .... unto thee	A
10	the more cheerfully.	cheerfully
14	which are written in the law and in the prophets.	which are according to the law and which are written in the prophets.
18	Whereupon certain Jews from Asia	amidst which they
—	nor with tumult	nor yet with tumult; but there were certain Jews from Asia—

CHAPTER XXV.

2	the high priest	the chief priests
5	any wickedness	any thing amiss
8	he .	Paul
16	deliver any man to die	give up any man
20	because I doubted of such manner of questions,	being perplexed how to inquire concerning these things,

Chapter XXVI.

28	Almost thou persuadest me to be a Christian.	with but little persuasion thou wouldest fain make me a Christian.
29	that not only thou, but also all that hear me this day, were both almost, and altogether	that whether with little or with much, not thou only, but .... might become

[Reddendum puto: 'I would pray to God, whether with little prayer or with much, that not' &c.]

Chapter XXVII.

14	Euroclydon.	Euraquilo.
19	we .... our own	they .... their own

Chapter XXVIII.

1	they .... they	we .... we
16	the centurion .... but.	A
25	our.	your
29	And when ... with themselves.	A
30	Paul	he

ROMANS.

Chapter I.

16	of Christ :	A
24	also.	A
29	fornication,	A
31	implacable,	A

Chapter II.

17	behold,	but if

Chapter III.

7	For if	But if
22	and upon all	A
30	seeing it is one God which shall justify	if so be that God is one, and he shall justify

SELECT TEXTUAL CORRECTIONS.

CHAPTER IV.

1	our father	our forefather
11	also:	A
15	for where	but where
19	he considered not	he considered
—	neither yet	and

CHAPTER V.

1	we have	let us have

CHAPTER VI.

11	our Lord	A
12	it in	A

CHAPTER VII.

6	that being dead wherein we were held;	having died to that wherein we were holden;
18	I find not.	is not.

CHAPTER VIII.

1	who walk .... spirit.	A
11	Christ	Christ Jesus
20-21	who hath subjected the same in hope, because the creature itself also	who subjected it, in hope that the creation itself also
24	for what a man seeth, why doth he yet hope for?	for who hopeth for that which he seeth?
26	infirmities	infirmity
34	that condemneth?	that shall condemn?
—	Christ	Christ Jesus
—	that is risen again	that was raised from the dead
—	even	A

CHAPTER IX.

28	For he ..... upon the earth.	For the Lord will execute his work upon the earth, finishing it and cutting it short.
31	hath not attained to the law of righteousness.	did not arrive at that law.
32	by the works of the law.	by works.
—	For.	A
33	whosoever	he that

K

Chapter X.

1	for Israel	for them
5	For Moses describeth the righteousness which is of the law, That the man which doeth those things shall live by them.	For Moses writeth that the man that doeth the righteousness which is of the law shall live thereby.
15	that preach the gospel of peace, and	A
17	of God	of Christ

Chapter XI.

6	But if . . . . work. . .	A
13	For	But
17	root and fatness . . .	root of the fatness
19	The branches	Branches
21	take heed lest he also spare not thee.	neither will he spare thee.
22	thee, goodness, . . .	thee, God's goodness,
31	may obtain	may now obtain

Chapter XII.

20	Therefore if	But if

Chapter XIII.

3	good works, ...	the good work,
9	Thou shalt not bear false witness	A
11	for us	for you

Chapter XIV.

4	God	the Lord
6	and he that . . . regard it. .	A
—	He that eateth . . .	and he that eateth,
9	and rose, and revived, . .	and lived again,
10	of Christ	of God
21	or is offended, or is made weak.	A
22	Hast thou faith . . .	The faith which thou hast,

Chapter XV.

7	us	you
8	Now I say that Jesus Christ .	For I say that Christ
15	brethren, ...	A
16	of Jesus Christ . . .	of Christ Jesus
17	whereof I may glory through Jesus Christ . . .	my glorying in Christ Jesus
18	of any of those things which Christ hath not wrought by me,	of any things save those which Christ wrought through me,
19	in the power of the Spirit of God;	in the power of the Holy Ghost;
24	I will come to you; . .	A
29	of the gospel	A

Chapter XVI.

3	Priscilla	Prisca
5	of Achaia	of Asia
6	on us.	on you.
8	Amplias	Ampliatus
16	The churches	All the churches
18	Jesus	A
24	The grace . . . . Amen. . .	A
27	be the glory	[to whom] be the glory

I CORINTHIANS.

Chapter I.

15	I had baptized . . .	ye were baptized
20	this world ?	the world ?
22	a sign, ...	signs,
23	unto the Greeks . . .	unto Gentiles
26	ye see	behold
29	in his presence. . . .	before God.
30	of God is made unto us wisdom,	was made unto us wisdom from God,

Chapter II.

1	testimony	mystery
4	of man's wisdom, . . .	of wisdom,
7	the world	the worlds

9	Eye	Things which eye
—	the things which . . .	Whatsoever things
13	the Holy Ghost . . .	the Spirit

Chapter III.

3	and divisions, ...	A
4	carnal ?	men ?
5	Who then is Paul, and who is Apollos, but ministers	What then is Apollos, and what is Paul ? Ministers,

Chapter IV.

2	Moreover	Here moreover
6	to think of men above . .	to go beyond

Chapter V.

1	commonly	actually
—	is not so much as named .	is not even
3	as	A
4	Jesus Christ (2) . . .	Jesus
7	for us :	A
12	Therefore	A

Chapter VI.

4	set them	do ye set them
7	Now therefore there is utterly a fault among you,	Nay, already it is altogether a defect in you,
20	and in your spirit, which are God's.	A

Chapter VII.

3	due benevolence : . . .	her due :
5	fasting and	A ·

Chapter VIII.

4	other	A
7	with conscience of the idol unto this hour eat it as a thing	being used until now to the idol, eat as of a thing
11	through thy knowledge shall the weak brother perish,	through thy knowledge he that is weak perisheth, the brother

SELECT TEXTUAL CORRECTIONS.

CHAPTER IX.

1	Am I not an apostle? am I not free?	Am I not free? am I not an apostle?
—	Christ	A
10	he that ploweth should plow in hope; and he that thresheth in hope should be partaker of his hope.	because he that ploweth ought to plow in hope; and he that thresheth to thresh in hope of partaking.
18	of Christ	A
20	as under the law . . .	as under the law, not being myself under the law,
22	as	A
23	this I do	I do all things

CHAPTER X.

1	Moreover	For
9	Christ, ...	the Lord,
9, 10	also	A
19	that the idol is any thing, or that which is offered in sacrifice to idols is any thing?	that a thing sacrificed to idols is anything, or that an idol is anything?
23	for me (2)	A
28	unto idols, ...	A
—	for the earth is the Lord's, and the fulness thereof: . .	A

CHAPTER XI.

2	brethren, ...	A
24	Take, eat:	A
—	broken	A
26	this cup	the cup
29	unworthily	A
—	not discerning the Lord's body.	if he discern not the body.
31	For if we would judge ourselves,	But if we discerned ourselves,
34	And if	If

CHAPTER XII.

2	ye were Gentiles, . . .	when ye were Gentiles,
—	carried away	ye were led away
3	calleth Jesus accursed; . .	saith Jesus is anathema;
—	that Jesus is the Lord, . .	Jesus is Lord,

8	knowledge by	knowledge according to
9	healing by the same Spirit ; .	healing in the one Spirit ;
12	of that one body, . . .	of the body,
13	into one Spirit. . . .	of one Spirit.
15, 16	is it therefore not of the body ?	it is not therefore not of the body.
30	best	greater

Chapter XIV.

18	my God, ...	God,
25	and thus	A
34	your women	the women
—	they are commanded to be .	let them be
35	women	a woman
37	commandments . . .	commandment

Chapter XV.

20	and become	A
29	for the dead (second) . .	for them
32	what advantageth it me, if the dead rise not? let us	what doth it profit me? if the dead are not raised, let us
44	there is	if there is
47	the Lord	A
55	O death, where is thy sting ? O grave, where is thy victory ?	O death, where is thy victory? O death, where is thy sting ?

Chapter XVI.

22	Jesus Christ	A ·
—	Anathema Maran-atha. . .	anathema. Maran atha.

2 CORINTHIANS.

Chapter I.

6	which is . . . . salvation. · .	or whether we be comforted, it is for your comfort, which worketh in the patient enduring of the same sufferings which we also suffer:
10	doth deliver :	will deliver :
12	simplicity	holiness
14	the Lord	our Lord

SELECT TEXTUAL CORRECTIONS.   135

18	was not	is not
20	all the promises of God in him are yea, and in him Amen,	how many soever be the promises of God, in him is the yea : wherefore also through him is the Amen,

Chapter II.

5	me, but in part : that I may not overcharge you all.	not to me, but in part (that I press not too heavily) to you all.

Chapter III.

3	in fleshy tables of the heart. .	in tables that are hearts of flesh.
10	For even	For verily

Chapter IV.

6	who commanded the light to shine	that said, Light shall shine
10	the Lord	A
14	by	with

Chapter V.

5	who also hath given . .	who gave
12	for	A
14	if one	one
17	all things	they
18	Jesus	A
21	For	A

Chapter VI.

16	ye are	we are

Chapter VII.

12	our care for you . . .	your earnest care for us
13	Therefore we were comforted in your comfort : yea, and	Therefore we have been comforted : and in our comfort
16	therefore	A

Chapter VIII.

4	that we would receive the gift, and take upon us	in regard of this grace and
4-5	saints. And this they did,	saints: and this,
19	with this grace,	in the matter of this grace,
—	same	A
—	and .... of your ready mind:	and to shew our readiness:
20	no man	any man
21	providing	for we take thought

Chapter IX.

4	this same confident boasting..	this confidence.
10	both minister.	shall supply

Chapter X.

7	do ye look	ye look
8	somewhat more	somewhat abundantly

Chapter XI.

1	a little in my folly :.	in a little foolishness:
3	so	A
—	simplicity	simplicity and purity
6	we have been throughly made manifest among you	we have made it manifest among all men to you-ward
31	our Lord Jesus Christ,	the Lord Jesus,
33	desirous to apprehend me :	in order to take me :

Chapter XII.

1	It is not expedient for me doubtless to glory.	I must needs glory, though it is not expedient; but
7	(*Probably corrupt. See note.*[1])	
11	in glorying	A
15	though the more abundantly I love you, the less I be loved.	If I love you more abundantly, am I loved the less?
19	Again, think ye	Ye think all this time
20	debates, envyings,	strife, jealousy,
—	strifes,	factions,

[1] In xii. 7 very ancient corruption seems to lurk. The διό (wherefore), which interrupts the construction, is supported by preponderant authority of mss., but is found in one version only. The repetition of the clause ἵνα μὴ ὑπεραίρωμαι has strong support in mss., but not so large as διό has.

Chapter XIII.

2	I write	A
4	though	A
7	I pray	we pray
14	Amen.	A

GALATIANS.
Chapter I.

10	for if	if
11	But	For
18	Peter, ...	Cephas, (so ii. 11, 14)

Chapter II.

14	why	how
16	knowing	yet knowing

Chapter III.

1	that ye should not obey the truth, ...	A
—	among you ? . . .	A
12	The man that	He that
17	in Christ	A
29	and heirs	heirs

Chapter IV.

6	your hearts, ...	our hearts,
7	of God through Christ. . .	through God.
14	my temptation which was in my flesh	that which was a temptation to you in my flesh
15	Where is then the blessedness ye spake of?	Where then is that gratulation of yourselves?
24	the two	two
25	and is	for she is
26	the mother of us all. . .	our mother.

Chapter V.

1	Stand fast therefore in the liberty wherewith Christ hath made us free,	With freedom did Christ set us free: stand fast therefore,
19	Adultery, ...	A
21	murders, ...	A
24	Christ's	of Christ Jesus

Chapter VI.

15	in Christ Jesus	A
—	availeth	is
17	the Lord	A

EPHESIANS.
Chapter I.

6	wherein he made us accepted	which he freely bestowed on us
15	and love unto all the saints,	and which you show toward all the saints, (? See Col. i. 4)
18	understanding	heart

Chapter II.

1	trespasses	your trespasses
17	to them	peace to them
19	but	but ye are

Chapter III.

3	he made known	was made known
6	of his promise in Christ	of the promise in Christ Jesus
8	among	unto
9	fellowship	dispensation
—	by Jesus Christ :	A
14	of our Lord Jesus Christ,	A
21	by Christ Jesus	and in Christ Jesus

Chapter IV.

6	in you all.	in all.
9	first	A
17	other Gentiles	the Gentiles

Chapter V.

2	loved us,	loved you,
5	ye know	ye know of a surety,
15	See then that ye walk circumspectly,	Look therefore carefully how ye walk,
17	understanding	understand
29	the Lord	Christ
30	of his flesh and of his bones.	A

SELECT TEXTUAL CORRECTIONS. 139

CHAPTER VI.

10	my brethren, ...	A
12	of the darkness of this world, .	of this darkness,

PHILIPPIANS.
CHAPTER I.

1	Jesus Christ, ...	Christ Jesus,
14	the word	the word of God
16-17	(*The contents of these verses*	*are transposed in Revised V.*)
18	notwithstanding . . .	only that
23	which is far better : . .	for it is very far better :
28	but to you of salvation, . .	but of you salvation,

CHAPTER II.

9	a name	the name
21	which are Jesus Christ's . .	of Jesus Christ.
30	not regarding	hazarding

CHAPTER III.

16	Nevertheless, whereto we have already attained, let us walk by the same rule, let us mind the same thing.	Only, whereunto we have already attained, by that same rule let us walk. (See p. 78.)

CHAPTER IV.

13	through Christ which . .	in him that
23	The grace of our Lord Jesus Christ be with you all. Amen.	The grace of the Lord Jesus Christ be with your spirit.

COLOSSIANS.
CHAPTER I.

2	and the Lord Jesus Christ. .	A
6	which is come unto you, as it is in all the world; and bringeth forth fruit, as it doth also in you, . . .	which is come unto you; even as it is also in all the world bearing fruit and increasing, as it doth in you also,
14	through his blood, . . .	A
16	that are (2)	A
23	to every creature . . .	in all creation
28	Jesus	A

Chapter II.

2	being knit	they being knit
—	to the acknowledgment of the mystery of God, and of the Father, and of Christ ;	that they may know the mystery of God, even Christ,
7	therein with thanksgiving. .	in thanksgiving.
11	of the sins	A
13	in	through
—	having forgiven you . .	having forgiven us
18	intruding into those things which he hath not seen, .	dwelling in the things which he hath seen,

Chapter III.

7	in them.	in these things.
13	Christ	the Lord
15	of God	of Christ
17	and the Father . . .	the Father
18	own	A
20	unto	in
22	God :	the Lord :
24	for ye serve	ye serve
25	But he that.	For he that

Chapter IV.

8	that he might know your estate, and	that ye may know our estate, and that he may
12	Christ, ...	Christ Jesus,
—	complete	fully assured
13	a great zeal	much labour
18	Amen.	A

1 THESSALONIANS.

Chapter I.

1	from God . . . . Christ . .	A
4–5	knowing, brethren beloved, your election of God. For	knowing, brethren beloved of God, your election, how that
5	we were among you . .	we shewed ourselves toward you

Chapter II.

9	for labouring	working
10	among you	toward you
15	their own prophets, . .	the prophets,
19	Christ	A

Chapter III.

2	and our fellowlabourer . .	A
11, 13	Christ	A

Chapter IV.

1	God, so ye	God, even as ye do walk,—that ye
8	who hath also given unto us his holy Spirit.	who giveth his Holy Spirit unto you.
11	own	A
13	I	we

Chapter V.

3	For when	When
5	Ye are all	for ye are all
27	holy	A
28	Amen.	A

2 THESSALONIANS.

Chapter I.

2	our Father	the Father
8	Christ :	A
12	Christ (1)	A

Chapter II.

2	of Christ	of the Lord
4	as God	A
6	in his time.	in his own season.
8	the Lord shall consume . .	the Lord Jesus shall slay
10	in them	for them
11	shall send	sendeth
16	even	A
17	you in every good word and work.	them in every good work and word.

Chapter III.

4	command you.	command.
12	by our	in the
14	and have	that ye have
18	Amen.	A

1 TIMOTHY.

Chapter I.

1	and Lord Jesus Christ, which is our hope.	and Christ Jesus our hope.
2	our Father and Jesus Christ	the Father and Christ Jesus
4	godly edifying.	a dispensation of God
12	And I thank	I thank
17	wise	A

Chapter II.

3	For.	A
7	in Christ.	A

Chapter III.

3	not given to wine,	no brawler,
—	not greedy of filthy lucre;	A
4	a brawler,	contentious,
16	God	He who

Chapter IV.

6	Jesus Christ,	Christ Jesus,
10	suffer reproach,	strive,
12	in spirit,	A

Chapter V.

4	good and.	A
16	man or	A
21	the Lord Jesus Christ,	Christ Jesus,

Chapter VI.

5	Perverse disputings	wranglings
—	from such withdraw thyself.	A
7	and it is certain	A
12	also	A
17	the living	A
19	eternal life.	the life which is life indeed.
21	Amen.	A

2 TIMOTHY.

Chapter I.

1, 10	Jesus Christ	Christ Jesus
3-4	in my prayers night and day; greatly desiring to see thee,	in my supplications, night and day longing to see thee,
11	of the Gentiles.	A

Chapter II.

3	Thou therefore endure hardness,	Suffer hardship with me,
—	Jesus Christ.	Christ Jesus.
7	and the Lord give thee	for the Lord shall give thee
19	of Christ .	of the Lord
21	and meet.	meet

Chapter III.

10	hast fully known	didst follow

Chapter IV.

1	the Lord Jesus Christ,	Christ Jesus,
14	reward him	the Lord will render to him
18	And the Lord .	The Lord
22	Jesus Christ	A
—	Amen.	A

TITUS.

Chapter I.

4	the Lord Jesus Christ	Christ Jesus
7	not given to wine,	no brawler,
—	not given to filthy lucre;	not greedy of filthy lucre;

Chapter II.

7	sincerity .	A

Chapter III.

1	and powers,	to authorities,
15	Amen.	A

PHILEMON.

2	to our beloved Apphia, . .	to Apphia our sister,
6	Jesus.	A
12	whom I have sent again : thou therefore receive him, that is, mine own bowels :	whom I have sent back to thee in his own person, that is my very heart :
20	refresh my bowels in the Lord.	refresh my heart in Christ.
25	Amen.	A

HEBREWS.

Chapter I.

2	in these last days . . .	in the end of these days
3	when he had by himself purged our sins,	when he had made purification of sins,
8	the sceptre . . .	and a sceptre
12	and they	As a garment, and they

Chapter III.

1	Christ Jesus ;	even Jesus ;
9	when your fathers tempted me, proved me,	wherewith your fathers tempted me by proving me,
10	that	this
16	for some . . . . provoke . .	For who . . . . provoke ?
—	howbeit not all . . . . Moses.	nay, did not all they . . . Moses ?

Chapter IV.

2	not being mixed with faith in them	because they were not united by faith with them
7	as it is said, . . .	as it hath been before said,

Chapter V.

4	he that is	when he is
12	that one teach you again which be the first principles	again that some one teach you the rudiments of the first principles

Chapter VI.

4	who were once enlightened, and have tasted . . .	who were once enlightened and tasted (? *once were*)
10	labour of love	the love

SELECT TEXTUAL CORRECTIONS.

Chapter VII

4	even	A
14	priesthood.	priests.
17	he testifieth,	it is witnessed of him,
18–19	For the law made nothing perfect, but the	(for the law made nothing perfect), and a
21	after the order of Melchisedec:	A
22	by so much	by so much also

Chapter VIII.

2	and not	not
4	priests	those
11	his neighbour	his fellow-citizen
12	and their iniquities	A

Chapter IX.

9	then present, in which	now present; according to which (i.e. *parable*)
10	which stood only in meats and drinks, and divers washings, and carnal ordinances,	being only (with meats and drinks and diverse washings) carnal ordinances,
17	otherwise it is of no strength at all	for doth it ever avail....?
28	so Christ.	so Christ also,

Chapter X.

1	can.	they can
2	offered?....sins.	offered,....sins?
7	O God.	A
12	this man.	he
16	minds	mind
30	saith the Lord.	A
34	of me in my bonds,	on them that were in bonds,
—	knowing in yourselves that ye have in heaven a better and an enduring substance.	knowing that ye yourselves have a better possession and an abiding one.
38	the just	my righteous one

L

Chapter XI.

3	things which are seen	what is seen
11	and was delivered of a child	A
13	and were persuaded of them	A
20	concerning	even concerning
32	and of (*three*)	A A A

Chapter XII.

3	himself,	themselves (?)
7	if ye endure chastening,	It is for chastening ye endure; (*see margin*)
15	many	the many
17	rejected : for he found no place of repentance, though	rejected (for he found no place of repentance), though
20	or thrust through with a dart.	A
24	better things	better
25	who	when they
—	if we	who
26	I shake	will I make to tremble
28	godly fear :	awe :

Chapter XIII.

6	and	A
—	fear what man shall do unto me.	fear. What shall man do unto me?
9	about	away
20	our Lord Jesus, that great	the great
—	through	with
—	covenant .	covenant, even our Lord Jesus,
21	work	thing
—	in you	in us

JAMES.

Chapter I.

19	Wherefore,	Ye know this,
—	let	But let
25	he	A

Chapter II.

3	here under	sit under
19	that there is one God ;	that God is one ;

SELECT TEXTUAL CORRECTIONS. 147

CHAPTER III.

5	how great a matter a little fire kindleth !	how much wood is kindled by how small a fire !
6	a world of iniquity : so is the tongue among our members, that it &c.	the world of iniquity among our members is the tongue, which &c.
8	unruly	restless
12	so can no fountain both yield salt water and fresh.	neither can salt water yield sweet.

CHAPTER IV.

4	adulterers and	A
5	The spirit that dwelleth in us lusteth to envy ?	doth the spirit which he made to dwell in us long unto envying ? (*See margin*)
11	and (1)	or
12	There is one lawgiver, . .	One only is the lawgiver and judge,
—	another ?	thy neighbour ?
14	For what is your life ? It is even	What is your life ? for ye are

CHAPTER V.

5	as	A
9	condemned :	judged :
11	endure.	endured :
16	Confess	Confess therefore
—	faults	sins

1 PETER.

CHAPTER I.

7	much	A
12	unto us	unto you
16	Be ye	Ye shall be
20	in these last times . . .	in the end of the times
22	through the Spirit . . .	A
—	with a pure heart . . .	from the heart
23	for ever.	A
24	of man	thereof
—	the flower thereof . . .	the flower

L 2

APPENDIX III

Chapter II.

6	Wherefore also . . .	Because
12	shall	A
21	for us, leaving us . . .	for you, leaving you
25	as sheep going astray . .	going astray like sheep

Chapter III.

8 having compassion one of another, love as brethren, be pitiful, be courteous ; | compassionate, loving as brethren, tender-hearted, humble-minded ;
9 knowing that ye are thereunto called, . . . | for hereunto were ye called,
15 the Lord God in your hearts : | in your hearts Christ as Lord :
16 whereas they speak evil of you, as of evildoers, . . . | wherein ye are spoken against,
20 once . . . . . | A
21 The like figure whereunto even baptism doth also now save us | which after a true likeness doth now save you, even baptism,

Chapter IV.

1	for us	A
3	of our life	A
—	us	A
8	shall cover the . . .	covereth a
14	on their part he is evil spoken of, but on your part he is glorified.	A
16	on this behalf. . . .	in this name.

Chapter V.

2 willingly ; . . . . | willingly, according unto God ;
5 be subject one to another, and be clothed with humility : | gird yourselves with humility, to serve one another ;
10 Jesus . . . . . | A
— make you perfect, stablish, strengthen, settle you. | shall himself perfect, stablish, strengthen you.
11 glory and . . . . | A
12 wherein ye stand. . . . | stand ye fast therein.
14 Jesus. Amen. . . . | A

2 PETER.

Chapter I.

3	to glory and virtue.	by his own glory and virtue.
21	holy men of God spake	men spake from God

Chapter II.

2	pernicious ways;	lascivious doings;
12	as natural brute beasts, made	as creatures without reason, born mere animals
—	speak evil of the things that they understand not; and shall utterly perish in their own corruption;	railing in matters whereof they are ignorant, shall in their destroying surely be destroyed,
13	and shall receive the reward of unrighteousness, as they that	suffering wrong as the hire of wrong-doing; men that
—	sporting themselves with their own deceivings while they feast with you;	revelling in their love-feasts while they feast with you;
15	Bosor	Beor.
17	clouds	and mists
—	to whom the mist of darkness is reserved for ever.	for whom the blackness of darkness hath been reserved.
18	that were clean escaped	who are just escaping

Chapter III.

3	there shall come in the last days scoffers,	in the last days mockers shall come with mockery,
10	in the night	A

1 JOHN.

Chapter I.

4	write we unto you, that your joy may be full.	we write, that our joy may be fulfilled.

Chapter II.

7	Brethren,	Beloved,
27	the same anointing	his anointing
—	ye shall abide .	ye abide
28	when he shall appear,	if he shall be manifested,

Chapter III.

1	of God :	of God : and such we are :
5	to take away our sins ; . .	to take away sins ;
14	his brother	A
16	the love of God . . .	love

Chapter IV.

3	that Jesus Christ is come in the flesh	Jesus
20	how can he love . . .	cannot love

Chapter V.

7	in heaven . . . . are one. .	A
8	and there are three that bear witness in earth, . . .	A
13	that believe on the name of the Son of God ; . . .	A
20	may know	know
21	Amen.	A

2 JOHN.

3	the Lord	A
8	we lose . . . we receive . .	ye lose . . . ye receive
9	transgresseth	goeth onward
—	he that abideth in the doctrine of Christ . . .	he that abideth in the teaching,
13	Amen.	A

3 JOHN.

5	to the brethren, and to strangers ;	toward them that are brethren and strangers withal ;
7	for his name's sake . .	for the sake of the Name
9	I wrote	I wrote somewhat
13	many things to write, . .	many things to write unto thee,

JUDE.

3	our common	the common
19	separate themselves, . .	make separations,
22	making a difference ; . .	who are in doubt ;

23	and others save with fear, pulling them out of the fire;	and some save, snatching them out of the fire; and on some have mercy with fear;
25	wise	A
—	and power both now and ever.	and power before all time, and now, and for evermore.

REVELATION.

Chapter I.

2	and of all things . . .	even of all things
6	kings and priests . . .	to be a kingdom, to be priests
8	the beginning and the ending;	A
—	the Lord, ...	the Lord God,
9	Jesus Christ (*bis*) . . .	Jesus (*bis*)
11	I am . . . . and, . . .	A
13	seven	A
18	Amen;	A
—	of hell and	A
20	candlesticks which thou sawest	candlesticks

Chapter II.

7	the midst of	A
9, 13	works, and . . .	A
15	, which thing I hate. . .	in like manner.
20	to teach and to seduce . .	and she teacheth and seduceth
21	of her fornication; and she repented not.	and she willeth not to repent of her fornication.
27	shall they be broken . .	are broken

Chapter IV.

10	fall down . . . . worship . . . . cast	shall fall down . . . . shall worship . . . . shall cast

Chapter V.

14	him that liveth for ever and ever.	A

Chapter VI.

1, 3, 5, 7	and see.	A
15	the mighty men, . . .	the strong,

Chapter VII.

5-8	were sealed	A (except Judah and Benjamin).

Chapter X.

5	his hand	his right hand

Chapter XI.

15	the kingdoms (*bis*) . . .	the kingdom
—	are become	is become
17	and art to come . . .	A

Chapter XII.

12	woe to the inhabiters of the earth and of the sea!	woe for the earth and for the sea:
17	of Jesus Christ. . . .	of Jesus.

Chapter XIV.

5	guile:	lie:
—	before the throne of God. .	A
8	Babylon is fallen, is fallen, that great city,	fallen, fallen is Babylon the great,
9	a third angel	another angel, a third,

Chapter XV.

3, 4, 8, 10, 12, 17	angel . .	A

Chapter XVI.

5	O Lord, ...	A
—	and wast, and shalt be, . .	and which wast, thou Holy One,
7	another out of the altar say, .	the altar saying,
16	Armageddon	Har Magedon.
17	of heaven, ...	A

Chapter XVII.

4	and filthiness	, even the unclean things
8	that was, and is not, and yet is.	how that he was, and is not, and shall come.
13	shall give	give

Chapter XVIII.

2	mightily with a strong voice, .	with a mighty voice,
13	cinnamon, ...	cinnamon, and spice,

SELECT TEXTUAL CORRECTIONS.

Chapter XIX.
13	dipped in	sprinkled with
17	supper of the great God ;	great supper of God ;

Chapter XXI.
27	that defileth,	unclean,

Chapter XXII.
1	a pure river	a river
—	of the Lamb.	of the Lamb, in the midst of the street thereof.
6	God of the holy prophets	God of the spirits of the prophets
11	be unjust	do unrighteousness
—	be filthy	be made filthy
—	be righteous	do righteousness
—	be holy	be made holy
20	Even so, come, Lord Jesus.	Come, Lord Jesus.
21	with you all.	with the saints.

The foregoing are but a small selection of the numerous variations exhibited by the mss. of the Apocalypse. They seem to be the most signal.

In using this Index it must be understood—

(1) That all, or nearly all, the changes noted are such as arose from new readings of the Greek text.

(2) That a vast number of new readings are omitted, which seem to make no signal change in the sense.

Many changes of small importance are recorded in this Index, I am quite sure. I can but express my earnest hope, that none of notable importance have been omitted through oversight.

POSTSCRIPT.

I HAD corrected the proof of my prefatory letter to Dr. Scrivener, and this final sheet of my Index was before me, when the new number (304) of the 'Quarterly Review' was brought into my study. Its opening article, on the Revised Greek Text, I read on the same evening, and again the following day. I read it without amazement, for certain reasons; but I read it also without amusement. The 'furor theologicus' never amuses, it only saddens me. I know what it has done in the ages past; I see what it is doing in the present day; I dread what it may do in the times that are coming. But many there are of two classes who will be more than amused; they will be delighted by the reviewer's unsparing onslaught. What classes I mean his acute mind may easily discern, and I leave him to consider the respective grounds of their delight.

The vials of the reviewer's wrath are chiefly emptied on the textual criticism of Dr. Westcott and Dr. Hort. That criticism, I own, did often decide the judgment of the revising company, but, in disputed cases, always after arguments on the different sides heard with careful attention. The reviewer, 'non videns manticæ quod in tergo est,' imputes to these two divines a magisterial tone and language (p. 360). But he seems (if I do not mistake him) to admit—and much of what he has said tends to prove—that he has not accurately mastered the critical principles of these eminently learned and indefatigably laborious scholars.

I do not notice this review with any purpose of formally replying to its assault upon the work of revision. Even if time and space allowed, I have neither the authority nor the minute textual learning which would justify me in attempting that task. But something I must say in reference to my second sermon. And I think the language used by the reviewer in his opening pages calls for that brief notice which this occasion offers.[1]

The facts of our work, simply and shortly stated, are these :—

In May 1870 the Southern Convocation, which is the larger fraction of the Anglican Church, nominated a committee to provide a revision of the Authorised Version of the Bible. This committee, from itself as a nucleus, formed two revising companies, and co-opted other members into each. The Presses of our two ancient Universities purchased the copyright of the entire work. The New Testament Company, of which alone I can speak, carried on its labours for eleven years, losing two by death, and co-opting one new member. The Presses published the Revised New Testament in May last, and when it was presented to the Southern Convocation, it was received with a vote of thanks to the Company—that Company consisting of one archbishop, several bishops, deans, archdeacons, and other Christian ministers.

Of such a work and such workmen the 'Quarterly' reviewer thinks it consistent with the Christian character, and not beneath his personal dignity, to suggest (p. 307) that they are committing 'assault and battery' on 'the very citadel of revealed truth ;' that 'it is high time *for every*

---

[1] I am bound to state that the *italics*, in what follows, are all my own, and that my use of them has obliged me, once or twice, to neglect those of the reviewer, but, I hope and believe, without injury to his meaning.

faithful man to bestir himself,' 'ne quid detrimenti civitas Dei capiat;' that 'such as have made Greek textual criticism *in any degree* their study, should address themselves to the investigation of the claims of this, the latest product of the combined Biblical learning of the Church and of the sects.'

Language like this can affect the revisers in one way only; it must make them sorry that the writer should have used it. The effects of it on himself become manifest in the sentences which next follow. He has overlooked the real circumstances of the case. He goes on to say that the authors of this new revision of the Greek text 'must experience at the hands of the Church nothing short of stern and well-merited rebuke.' The rebuke which these prelates and others *have* received is a vote of thanks from the Southern House of Convocation. 'No middle course' (so he goes on) ' presents itself, since *assuredly* to construct a new Greek text formed no part of the instructions which the *revisionists* received *at the hands of the Committee of the Southern Province.*' If the reviewer had carefully read and remembered the Preface of the Revised New Testament, he would have spared himself this signal error. The Committee was, as I have said, itself the nucleus of the revising company, the co-opting body, the guide and guardian (so to say) of our initial acts; and as we began, so we went on to the close. That Committee had received from Convocation itself the instruction 'that the revision be so conducted as to comprise both marginal renderings and such *emendations* as it may be found necessary to insert *in the text* of the Authorised Version.' But I return to our reviewer. ' Rather,' he adds, 'were they warned against venturing on such an experiment,' the fundamental principle of the entire undertaking having been declared at the outset to be that 'a revision of the Authorised Version is desirable,' and the fundamental rule laid down for the revising body being that they should introduce into the text as few alterations 'as possible consistent with faithfulness.' Error here grows out of error; the resolution of Convocation itself that revision is desirable is confused with the first 'by-law' framed by the Committee 'to introduce' &c. He then proceeds: 'It cannot, of course, be denied that this last clause set the door inconveniently wide open for innovation. But then a limit was prescribed to the amount of licence which might possibly result by the insertion of *a proviso, which, however, is found to have been disregarded by the revisionists almost entirely. The condition was imposed upon them, that, whenever decidedly preponderating evidence constrained their adoption of some change in the text from which the Authorised Version was made, they should indicate such alteration in the margin. Will it be believed that, this notwithstanding, not one of the many alterations which have been introduced into the original text is distinctly so commemorated?*'

Will it be believed that the clause setting open the door was the first by-law framed by the Committee for the guidance of itself after its strength should have been completed by co-optation? Will it be believed that the proviso requiring the marginal indication of every textual change was another by-law of the Committee for its own guidance when it should expand into a company—a law which they were at liberty to modify or abolish, if it eventually proved to be inconvenient? Will it be believed that in our Preface (iii. 1) it is distinctly said that it did prove inconvenient to record the changes in the margin, and that a better mode of giving them publicity was found—namely, the printing them in those two Greek texts which have now been edited and published by Archdeacon Palmer and Dr. Scrivener severally? Finally, will it be believed that either this reviewer has failed to read the Preface to the book which he lays under his anathema? or that he read it so cursorily as not to master its contents? or that, having read and mastered, he forgot them when he sat down to demolish the book, and so drew up an indictment, every count of which is an error?

I am prepared to expect that this philippic, when examined by experts, will be found throughout 'qualis ab incepto.' In the course of my experience in the Jerusalem Chamber, I never heard from my friend Dr. Scrivener, whom the reviewer proclaims to be 'facile princeps' in our company, any suggestion that the most ancient uncial codices are so contemptibly corrupt as to be unsafe guides in the constitution of a Greek text. Yet so the reviewer insists; while we are left to suppose (for he is not explicit on this point) that the few cursive MSS. on which his cherished 'textus receptus' (so called) mainly rests, are more trustworthy—MSS. having their parentage and growth in those *enlightened* times that lie between the death of Charlemagne and the Crusades, or transcribed from these in subsequent centuries, which, though not devoid of scholastic learning, were, in the Western Church, ignorant of Greek.[1]

I am compelled by this review to withdraw a statement on which I have ventured more than once, to the effect that the reading θεὸς in 1 Tim. iii. 16 is now abandoned by all Anglican divines. I really thought that when a divine at

[1] The only rule of textual criticism discoverable in this review is (317) that the text which has been 'in possession' for three centuries and a half should be let alone when the evidence for and against it is evenly balanced. If a corrupt text has been 'in possession' for ever so long through the timid negligence of authority, it has no just claim to be respected on that account. In any case, it is a mere truism to say that what stands should be left standing if no reason is shown for removing it. But where and how we are to find valid reasons, when they exist, this writer does not tell us. Dr. Scrivener has given four rules for that purpose (Intr. p. 484), which I commend to the attention of my readers. And of Cod. B he says (480): 'It is a document of such value that it grows by experience even upon those who may have been a little prejudiced against it, adding that its best associate is Cod. C, where the testimony of that precious palimpsest can be had.'

once so learned and so conservative as Bishop C. Wordsworth had forsaken it, there was no further chance of support for it in our Church. I find myself mistaken; for in this reviewer it finds an uncompromising champion, who would cry to the last, δίχα δ' ἄλλων μονόφρων εἰμί. Well, I have no room for the argument here, and I must be content with referring to its full statement in Dr. Scrivener's Introduction, 552-6. I will only add that when the reviewer calls μυστήριον . . . ὅς a 'patent absurdity,' he seems to have forgotten the facts of grammar. If μυστήριον means Christ (and it does), the reference to it by masc. ὅς is one of the simplest examples of synesis, a construction which abounds in Greek and Latin, and becomes, in this place, inevitable.

NOTE.

ON the eve of publication I have received the Philadelphian 'Sunday School Times' of Nov. 5, containing a paper on Westcott and Hort's Greek Testament, vol. i. I cannot refrain from citing here the main portion of it, as a wholesome antidote to the unfair and intemperate critique which has drawn forth my postscript.

'This edition of the Greek Testament will mark an epoch in the history of New Testament criticism. Dr. Schaff accepts its text enthusiastically as "the oldest and purest" which has yet been published. Many in England, and still more, probably, in Germany, will heartily welcome it as a work bearing everywhere the stamp of independent, original research, and the most painstaking care. But in some quarters it cannot fail to encounter deadly hostility, and before its conclusions are generally adopted there will be much discussion. Though the work will now be more fairly judged than if it had been published twenty years ago, the charge of extreme rashness will doubtless be brought against the editors by such critics as Dean Burgon and the Rev. J. B. McClellan; and Dr. Scrivener, who had the use of their "provisional" text, has already, in the second edition of his Introduction (1874), strongly expressed his dissent from many of their conclusions. Even scholars who have become emancipated from the superstitious worship of the so-called "received text," and who are ready to decide critical questions on purely critical principles, and not by their "infallible instincts," may be startled at the boldness of the editors in the use of the pruning-knife, which in their hands cuts deeper than even in those of Tischendorf and Tregelles. Westcott and Hort, for example, regard as later additions to the text not only the last twelve verses of Mark, the account of the descent of the angel into the pool of Bethesda (or "Bethzatha," as they read), and the story of the woman taken in adultery (John vii. 53 to viii. 11), but the passages noted in the margin of the

Revised Version, at Matt. xvi. 2, 3; Luke xxii. 19, 20, 43, 44; xxiii. 34; xxiv. 3, 6, 12, 36, 40, 51, 52; and John iii. 13, as "omitted by some [or "many"] ancient authorities." Other readings of theirs will seem to many, at first sight at least, very questionable.

'But the last charge which can be justly brought against the editors is that of rashness. They may have erred in judgment, but they have come to their conclusions with great deliberation. The history of the work entitles it, not, indeed, to immediate, unquestioning acceptance as final in its decisions, but to the most respectful consideration. It "was projected and commenced in 1853, and the work has never been laid more than partially aside in the interval, though it has suffered many delays and interruptions. The mode of procedure adopted by the editors from the first was to work out their results independently of each other, to hold no counsel together except upon results already provisionally obtained, and to discuss on paper the comparatively few points of initial difference until either agreement or final difference was reached." To this it may be added that a large part of the text, the Gospels at least, appears to have been in type for more than ten years, during which period it has been revised and re-revised with great care, as deeper investigations have led the editors to modify here and there their earlier decisions. As to the character of the editors, none who are acquainted with the writings of Professor Westcott and Dr. Hort will question their eminent intellectual and moral qualifications for the task they have undertaken,—the great moral qualification, in studies such as these, being the single aim to ascertain the truth.

'It is important, however, to observe that the present volume exhibits only the *results* of their critical investigations. It takes no notice of the text of any previous edition, so that there is nothing to show the extent of its divergence from the so-called "received text," or of its agreement with the great critical editions of Tischendorf and Tregelles, with which, notwithstanding many differences, it does agree in the main. There is no discussion of any reading, no statement of the authorities (manuscripts, &c.), which, in any questionable case, support the text. Alternative readings, indeed, are given, where the

editors regard the true reading as more or less uncertain ; also
certain noteworthy rejected readings appear in the text in
double brackets, or in the margin with certain marks ; and at
the end of the volume there is a list of still other rejected readings "which have been thought worthy of notice in the
appendix [to the second volume] on account of some special
interest attaching to them." This list also includes a few
passages in which the editors (or one of them) suspect "some
primitive error," and propose conjectural emendations. But it
is a mere list. There is also a very condensed sketch (pp. 541--
562) of the conclusions of the editors in regard to the true
principles of criticism, the history of the text, the grouping of
our chief documentary authorities in accordance with their
peculiar characteristics, and the determination of the relative
value of the several documents and groups of documents, in
estimating which "the history and genealogy of textual trans-
mission have been taken as the necessary foundation."

'It is the "critical introduction" in vol. ii. which will give
the edition of Westcott and Hort its distinctive value, and
which, whether all their conclusions prove firmly established or
not, will be most heartily welcomed by scholars, and cannot
fail to contribute greatly to the advancement of New Testament
criticism. They have undertaken a very difficult and delicate
task ; but their method is the true one. Some pioneering had
been done by Griesbach and others ; but no such comprehensive and scientific investigation of the character and relative
value of our external authorities for settling the text has been
hitherto attempted. It is on this introduction that the whole
structure of the editors rests ; and any criticism of particular
readings which they have adopted should in fairness be
reserved till the facts and reasonings on which their system
of criticism is founded have been carefully studied and
weighed.

'To describe the four types of text, "the Western," "the
Alexandrian," "the Neutral," and "the Syrian" (earlier and
later), which they find represented in our critical documents,
would require more space than can here be allowed. It may
be enough to say that the text which they designate as
"neutral" and regard as in general approximating most closely

to the original autographs, is represented in its greatest purity by the Vatican manuscript (B), to which they assign superlative value; the Sinaitic (Aleph) being, in their judgment, next in importance, but far less pure. But, "with certain limited classes of exceptions, the readings of Aleph and B combined may safely be accepted as genuine in the absence of specially strong internal evidence to the contrary, and can never be safely rejected altogether" (p. 557). Nay, every combination of B with one other primary manuscript, as in the gospels L, C, or T, " is found to have a large proportion of readings, which on the closest scrutiny have the ring of genuineness, and hardly any that look suspicious after full consideration." "Even when B stands alone, its readings must never be lightly rejected" (*ibid.*). This estimate differs somewhat from that of Professor T. R Birks of Cambridge, who conceives himself to have proved, by mathematical calculations, "that on the hypothesis most favourable to the early manuscripts, and specially to the Vatican, its weight is exactly that of two manuscripts of the fifteenth century, while the Sinaitic weighs only one-third more than an average manuscript of the eleventh century." (*Essay on the Right Estimation of Manuscript Evidence in the Text of the New Testament.* London, 1878, p. 66.)

'The present volume is issued in such a form that it may be used independently of the second : and it is apparently supposed that there will be some or many theological students whose want of a convenient manual edition will be met by this volume alone. It certainly is one which every theological student may well desire to possess, and should possess if possible ; but the question may arise how far it will serve as his only edition. If he is ready to accept the conclusions of the editors without further inquiry or examination of evidence, and without comparison with those of other critics, and if he does not care to have a text furnished with references to parallel or illustrative passages, or to the quotations from the Old Testament, this volume may be perfectly satisfactory. It is beautifully printed, though the type is not large ; the lines are well leaded ; its form is convenient ; and it may be read with great delight. Indeed, there is no other existing edition of the Greek Testament in which so much is done to aid the mind of the reader by the form in which the matter is presented to the eye. The great natural divisions of the larger books are marked by a wide space, and by the printing of the initial words in capitals ; the minor sub-divisions, but such as comprise many paragraphs, are separated by a smaller space ; the paragraphs, when they include a series of connected topics, as, for example, Matt. v. 17-48, are broken up by short but well-marked spaces into sub-paragraphs, as in Herbert Spencer's writings,—a most excellent device, worthy of general introduction. " Uncial type" is employed for quotations from the Old Testament, and also to mark phrases borrowed from it ; rhythmical passages, like Luke i. 46-55, 68-79, as well as poetical quotations from the Old Testament, are printed in a metrical form. The chapters and verses are numbered only in the margin. This sometimes leaves uncertainty as to the beginning of a verse, in which case the doubt should have been removed by a little mark of separation. For one who wishes to give himself to the continuous reading of the Greek text with the least possible distraction, this edition has no rival.'

No intelligent scholar, even though he may have other editions which will supply some of the deficiencies that have been mentioned, will be fully contented with the first volume alone. The second volume is really the basis of the first, and its necessary explanation ; it is that by which the value of the editors' work must be measured.

STANDARD WORKS
PUBLISHED BY
RICHARD BENTLEY & SON.

The HISTORY of ANTIQUITY. From the German of MAX
DUNCKER. By EVELYN ABBOTT, M.A., LL.D., of Balliol College, Oxford. The first
5 vols. are now published in demy 8vo. 21s. each.

The HISTORY of ROME. From the German of THEODOR
MOMMSEN, by the Rev. W. P. DICKSON. The Library Edition, 4 vols. demy 8vo. 75s.;
or the Popular Edition, 4 vols. crown 8vo. 46s. 6d.

The HISTORY of GREECE. From the German of ERNST CURTIUS.
By A. W. WARD, M.A. 5 vols. demy 8vo. 90s.

The RISE and PROGRESS of the ENGLISH CONSTITUTION. By
Sir EDWARD CREASY, late Chief Justice of Ceylon. Twelfth Edition. Crown 8vo. 7s. 6d.

The LIVES of the QUEENS of ENGLAND of the HOUSE of
HANOVER. By JOHN DORAN, F.S.A., Author of 'London in the Jacobite Times' &c.
Fourth and Enlarged Edition. 2 vols. demy 8vo. 25s.

The NAVAL HISTORY of GREAT BRITAIN (1793–1827). By
WILLIAM JAMES. With a Continuation by Captain CHAMIER. 6 vols. crown 8vo.
with Portraits, 36s.

The HISTORY of the AMERICAN CIVIL WAR. By Colonel
FLETCHER. 3 vols. demy 8vo. 54s.

The FIFTEEN DECISIVE BATTLES of the WORLD, from
Marathon to Waterloo. By Sir EDWARD CREASY, late Chief Justice of Ceylon. Library
Edition. Demy 8vo. 10s. 6d.; or the Popular Edition, the Twenty-seventh, cr. 8vo. 6s.

The HISTORY of the OTTOMAN TURKS, from the Beginning of
their Empire to the Close of 1878. By Sir EDWARD CREASY, late Chief Justice of
Ceylon. A New and Revised Edition, being the Fifth. Crown 8vo. 6s.

CURIOSITIES of NATURAL HISTORY. By FRANK BUCKLAND.
The Popular Edition. With Illustrations, in 4 vols. small crown 8vo. 14s. Each
Volume can be had separately, price 3s. 6d.

The HEAVENS: an Illustrated Handbook of Popular Astronomy.
By AMÉDÉE GUILLEMIN. Edited by J. NORMAN LOCKYER, F.R.A.S. Revised Edition.
Demy 8vo. with over 200 Illustrations, 12s.

ADAM and the ADAMITE; or, the Harmony of Scripture and
Ethnology. By DOMINICK MCCAUSLAND, Q.C. Crown 8vo. with Map, 6s.

SERMONS in STONES; or, Scripture confirmed by Geology.
By DOMINICK MCCAUSLAND, Q.C. New Edition, with Memoir of the Author. Crown
8vo. with 19 Illustrations, 6s.

The BUILDERS of BABEL; or, the Confusion of Languages. By
DOMINICK MCCAUSLAND, Q C. Crown 8vo. 6s.

ESSAYS, Classical and Theological. By the late CONNOP THIRL-
WALL, D.D., Bishop of St. David's. Edited by the Rev. Canon PEROWNE. Demy
8vo. 20s.

The CHURCH and its ORDINANCES. Sermons by the late
WALTER FARQUHAR HOOK, D.D., Dean of Chichester. Edited by the Rev. WALTER
HOOK, Rector of Porlock. 2 vols. demy 8vo. 10s. 6d.

The LIVES of the ARCHBISHOPS of CANTERBURY, from St.
Augustine to Juxon. By the late WALTER FARQUHAR HOOK, D.D., Dean of Chichester.
11 vols. demy 8vo. £8. 5s.

The LIFE and LETTERS of WALTER FARQUHAR HOOK, late
Dean of Chichester. Edited by the Rev. W. R. W. STEPHENS, Prebendary of Chichester,
&c. The Popular Edition, in 1 vol. crown 8vo. with Index and Portrait, 6s.

London: RICHARD BENTLEY & SON, 8 New Burlington Street,
Publishers in Ordinary to Her Majesty the Queen.

STANDARD WORKS
PUBLISHED BY
RICHARD BENTLEY & SON.

The **AUTOBIOGRAPHY of PRINCE METTERNICH.** 1773–1830.
Edited by his Son, Prince RICHARD METTERNICH. 5 vols. demy 8vo. with Portrait and Facsimiles, 90s.

The **LIFE of LORD PALMERSTON.** With Selections from his Diaries and Correspondence. By the Hon. EVELYN ASHLEY, M.P. The New Edition, 2 vols. crown 8vo. with Frontispiece to each volume, 12s.

LORD BEACONSFIELD: his Life, Character, and Works. From the German of GEORG BRANDES. By JANE STURGE. Demy 8vo. 6s.

CORRESPONDENCE OF TALLEYRAND AND LOUIS XVIII. DURING THE CONGRESS OF VIENNA. In 2 vols. demy 8vo. 24s.

MEMOIR of EARL SPENCER (Lord Althorp). By Sir DENIS LE MARCHANT, Bart. Demy 8vo. 16s.

HISTORICAL CHARACTERS: Talleyrand, Mackintosh, Cobbet, Canning, Peel. By Lord DALLING and BULWER. Fifth and Enlarged Edition. Crown 8vo. 6s.

A MEMOIR of CHARLES the TWELFTH of SWEDEN. By his Majesty OSCAR II. Translated, by special permission, by GEORGE APGEORGE, Her Britannic Majesty's Consul at Stockholm. Royal 8vo. with Two Illustrations, 12s.

The **FRENCH HUMORISTS from the TWELFTH to the NINE-TEENTH CENTURY.** By WALTER BESANT. M.A., Christ's Coll., Cambridge, Author of 'Studies in Early French Poetry,' &c. Demy 8vo. 15s.

The **LIVES of WITS and HUMORISTS.** By JOHN TIMBS, F.S.A. 2 vols. crown 8vo. with Portrait. 12s. The LIVES of the LATER WITS and HUMORISTS. In 2 vols. crown 8vo. 12s.

The **LIFE of OLIVER CROMWELL.** From the French of M. GUIZOT. By ANDREW SCOBLE. Crown 8vo. with Four Portraits, 6s.

The **LIFE of MARY QUEEN of SCOTS.** From the French of M. MIGNET. By ANDREW SCOBLE. Crown 8vo. with Two Portraits, 6s.

The **INGOLDSBY LEGENDS;** or, Mirth and Marvels. By Rev. RICHARD HARRIS BARHAM. The Annotated Edition, 2 vols. demy 8vo. Illustrated by Cruikshank and Leech, 24s. The Illustrated Edition, printed on toned paper, crown 4to. bevelled boards, gilt edges 21s.; or, in white binding, 22s. 6d. The Carmine Edition, with border line round each page, with Seventeen Illustrations, bevelled boards, gilt edges, 10s. 6d. The Burlington Edition, 3 vols. fcp 8vo 10s. 6d. The Edinburgh Edition, crown 8vo. with Thirty-two Engravings by Cruikshank, Leech, Tenniel, and Du Maurier, cloth, 6s. The (New) Popular Edition, crown 8vo. cloth, 3s. 6d. The Victoria (Pocket) Edition, in fcp. 8vo. cloth, 2s.

The **BENTLEY BALLADS.** Selected from 'Bentley's Miscellany.' Crown 8vo. 6s.

The **NOVELS of MISS FERRIER.** Library Edition, in 6 vols. 21s.; or each story. separately, 7s.

The **NOVELS of MISS AUSTEN.** The only Complete Edition. 6 vols. crown 8vo. with a Frontispiece to each volume, 36s.; or each volume separately, 6s.

The **WORKS of THOMAS LOVE PEACOCK.** The Collected Edition, including his Novels, Fugitive Pieces, Poems, &c. Edited by Sir HENRY COLE, K.C.B., and with Preface by Lord HOUGHTON. 3 vols. crown 8vo. with Portrait, 31s. 6d.

The **NOVELS of MISS BROUGHTON.** 7 vols. crown 8vo. 42s.; or each volume separately, 6s.

The **NOVELS of MRS. HENRY WOOD.** 27 vols. crown 8vo. £8. 2s.; or each volume separately, 6s.

London: RICHARD BENTLEY & SON, 8 New Burlington Street.
Publishers in Ordinary to Her Majesty the Queen.

www.ingramcontent.com/pod-product-compliance
Lightning Source LLC
Chambersburg PA
CBHW032138160426
43197CB00008B/694